The Tao of Open Source Intelligence

Stewart K. Bertram

The Tao of Open Source Intelligence

STEWART K. BERTRAM

IT Governance Publishing

IT Governance Publishing
IT Governance Limited
Unit 3, Clive Court
Bartholomew's Walk
Cambridgeshire Business Park
Ely
Cambridgeshire
CB7 4EA
United Kingdom
www.itgovernance.co.uk

First published in the United Kingdom in 2015
by IT Governance Publishing

ISBN 978-1-84928-728-9

FOREWORD

The Defence Intelligence Staff in London created an open source intelligence (OSINT) cell in 1993. In it were two civilian analysts with computers connected to the Internet over a 28K modem and a few subscriptions to databases and knowledge services. It was the personal initiative of a forward-thinking branch leader whose responsibility was ROW – the rest of the world. His problem was trying to provide intelligence and background on crises such as those in Sierra Leone, the Democratic Republic of the Congo and Bosnia, where the legacy of the giant Cold War information collection machine was not looking.

22 years later, the news in the UK was dominated by public dismay that the security services had not noticed that the Facebook pages of three teenage girls from Bethnal Green indicated their intention to travel to Syria to join ISIL at a time when GCHQ and the Home Office are on the defensive over their surveillance of social media and personal communications – thanks largely to the lethal revelations of Edward Snowden – the outrage over the security services' failure to identify what these three girls were saying in public shows the confusion that surrounds the world of OSINT.

Stewart Bertram brings experience of service within national intelligence, a rich computing science background, and the diligent, systematic, curious and imaginative mind of a professional intelligence analyst. This book cleverly distils the essence of his accumulated insight simply and clearly for the benefit of those who occasionally dabble in OSINT. It is also a valuable handbook for investigators who live in the surface, deep and dark webs.

Bertram describes the Internet as 'a forest of irrelevant babble' and this statement alone is a clue to where the commercial value of effective OSINT lies. Googling irrelevant babble is what a lot of people do while being paid. They are wasting company time. In any other business domain there would be standards, ethics, rules, process, tools and a dynamic training programme to maintain currency in the work force. We all perform data management – some do it very well – but when searching, collating, evaluating and understanding what people said, thought, perceived and intended, we can become impatient and frustrated by the volume and complexity of information sources, unsystematic and inefficient in our search and collation, and biased and narrow in our interpretation of what the extracted babble may mean in a particular context.

This book provides a logical framework to help improve every aspect of our thinking and practise of OSINT. By its very name – Tao – Bertram addresses aspects of the underlying natural order of OSINT. He offers the reader no specified doctrine, but rather an approach to the complexity of OSINT and some tools and techniques to help the reader get into the spirit of thinking laterally, thinking from a subject perspective, and thus detecting faint signals that elusive targets have inadvertently left. It is more art than science, but the Ying needs the Yang. Implicit in Tao is correct behaviour. Ethics and OSINT is not addressed here, but is a subject that any professional must engage with.

Bertram avoids telling us how much he knows about computing science, instead helpfully illustrating important aspects of theory by demonstrating the value of software tools and appealing to the natural human ability to relate to different types of imagery – the book is peppered with simple screen-shot examples from the many free tools available. He also uses case studies and boxed 'Talking Points' to add valuable context to every theme he addresses.

For investigators, as well as all of us who inadvertently reveal corporate intent in our unplanned surface web searches, the section on Internet privacy and surveillance is essential reading. Because we set our own preferences on our computers, we leave a trail via our unique IP address on every website we visit. This provides a lot of evidence for a skilled OSINT investigator. Understanding this opportunity from a target's and an investigator's perspective is part of the culture – the Tao – of OSINT.

The traditional and familiar culture of government intelligence agencies has formed around secret intelligence, high-security databases and bespoke analytical support systems. All of these are very expensive. There is recognition within the intelligence community that the bulk of intelligence used now comes from open sources but the crown jewels that give assurance to decision makers comes from secret sources. Secret intelligence may only represent 5% of the total but its value is 90%. However, since the Edward Snowden revelations, this balance of value is likely to be eroded in favour of OSINT. The free tools, special techniques and sheer volume of data available indicate that bespoke systems procured through the government will never keep pace with developments in the private sector. It is certain that training in new techniques will also fall behind skills requirements. It is my opinion that unless the government embraces OSINT properly, by accepting the skills and systems provided by the private sector, they will not be justifying their share of the national budget and the national security capability will be eroded. The commercial world is still slow on the uptake. Commerce understands business intelligence and the value of data, but it still needs some persuading that an art form like OSINT has real commercial value

Stewart Bertram's book is timely and indicative of the new world order for intelligence. The Open Source Intelligence Research Association (OSIRA) is a nascent global community of interest that seeks to share OSINT tactics, techniques and procedures to equip OSINT practitioners with best practice. As a founding speaker at OSIRA, Stewart Bertram makes another valuable contribution to this growing aspect of the information age.

Chris Holtom CBE
February 2015

PREFACE

Learn the tools and techniques of modern Open Source Intelligence (OSINT) in this authoritative but accessible work, which takes the reader beyond the front page of Google and into a rich new world of investigative possibilities.

Suitable for both novice and seasoned investigators alike, this work introduces the core concepts of OSINT in the information age through a blend of theory and practical exercises. Dealing in-depth with more than 30 freely available OSINT tools, this book seeks to quantifiably build the reader's skills within this rapidly emerging area of intelligence and investigative professional practice.

In addition to the introduction of the core tools and techniques, *The Tao of Open Source Intelligence* seeks to cut through the baffling array of technical terms often synonymous with the Internet. A rigorous definition of what terms such as Surface, Dark and Deep webs, meta search engines, social media and indexing among others are broken down and their relevance to the investigative process clearly explained.

Theoretical sections mixed with more practical text give a guide to the more complex issues associated with OSINT, such as the operational security, surveillance and counter surveillance in cyberspace and the issues associated with running covert human intelligence sources within the digital realm.

The Tao of Open Source Intelligence represents the current state of the art within this field and gives investigators new and old a solid foundation from which to build their own professional practices from.

Whether public or private sector, this work is comprehensive enough to give insight for a broad readership while specific enough to provide genuine guidance on key areas of OSINT professional practice.

ABOUT THE AUTHOR

Stewart K. Bertram is a career intelligence analyst, having spent more than a decade working across the fields of counter terrorism, cyber security, corporate investigations and geopolitical analysis. Holding both a Master's degree in Computing as well as a Master of Letters in Terrorism Studies, Stewart is uniquely placed at the cutting edge of intelligence and investigation, where technology and established tradecraft combine. Stewart fuses his academic knowledge with significant professional experience, having used OSINT on real-world topics as diverse as terrorist use of social media in Sub-Saharan Africa to threat assessment concerning the London Olympic Games. Stewart teaches courses on OSINT as well as practising what he preaches in his role as a cyber threat intelligence manager for some of the world's leading private sector intelligence and security agencies.

ACKNOWLEDGEMENTS

I would like to thank Chris Evans, ITSM Specialist, Giuseppe G. Zorzino CISA CGEIT CRISC, Security Architect, and ir. H.L. (Maarten) Souw RE, Enterprise Risk and QA Manager, UVW for their helpful comments during the review process.

DEDICATION

For my mum, Marianne. Because you always could see the
man that I could be, in the boy that I was…

Your son always, Stewart

CONTENTS

Contents

INTRODUCTION: "WHAT CAN OPEN SOURCE INTELLIGENCE DO FOR ME?"

…is probably the main question that you had in mind when you picked up this book.

After spending more than a decade working within the field of intelligence and security, and five years teaching open source intelligence (OSINT) techniques to hundreds of professionals within the military, police, counter fraud, academia, non-governmental organisation (NGO) and government sectors, I have been asked that question a thousand times and I can honestly say that I am no closer to giving an accurate answer now than when I was originally asked the question.

Although modern OSINT is many things, it's perhaps easier to fully conceptualise its capability by defining what OSINT is not. OSINT is not the silver bullet that will blow your stalled investigation wide open, and neither is it just another faddy 'must have' capability; it is certainly not a frightening and soulless computer-based technology that is here to take your job. Instead, OSINT is just another arrow within the quiver of the investigative analyst, just like techniques such as interviewing, surveillance, fingerprinting and any number of others open to the skilled professional investigator or analyst.

Wikipedia defines the term as:

> *"Open-source intelligence (OSINT) is intelligence collected from publicly available sources. In the intelligence community (IC), the term "open" refers*

Introduction: "What Can Open Source Intelligence Do For Me?"

to overt, publicly available sources (as opposed to covert or clandestine sources); "[1]

Based even on the loosest interpretation of the preceding definition, it is obvious that OSINT is not a new capability, given how accessible and easy to use it is. What has changed the game for OSINT is the arrival of the Internet.

Until usage of the Internet became widespread, OSINT was confined to primarily paper-based resources such as libraries and other common paper media such as newspapers, industry publications, fliers and propaganda. This 'old school' form of OSINT is of course useful for analysis and investigation; indeed anyone who has seen legendary Central Intelligence Agency analyst Sherman Kent's notebooks will testify that they are filled with newspaper clippings. However, older OSINT research was limited by both the coverage of its information and the ability of the researcher to focus the capability on a specific subject, be it a person, location or topic. In plain terms, with paper-based Open Source: what you saw was what you got and that was that.

What has changed this status quo is the arrival of the Internet, and particularly the explosion in the use of social media technology circa 2000. The rise of these two technologies created a multilingual, geographically distributed, completely unregulated publishing platform to which any user could also become an author and a publisher. The effect of this was to vastly expand both the coverage of the topics covered by OSINT and to increase the ability of the researcher to focus OSINT capabilities to predefined information requirements. By increasing the coverage and focus of OSINT the Internet

---

[1] *http://en.wikipedia.org/wiki/Open-source_intelligence#cite_note-1*

effectively promoted OSINT from a supporting role to finally sit alongside other more clandestine and less accessible investigative capabilities[5].

 Talking point: the *Internet* and *cyberspace*

Have you ever wondered what the difference (if any) is between the term 'cyberspace' and 'the Internet'? The term 'cyberspace' was popularised in the 1980s by the science fiction author William Gibson, in his seminal cyberpunk novels *Burning Chrome*[2] and *Neuromancer*[3]. Gibson's intent behind using the term 'cyberspace' was to encapsulate a number of fictional communication technologies as a foil for his books' plotlines. Later interpretations of what cyberspace actually was became more defined, with the Oxford English Dictionary currently defining the term as "The notional environment in which communication over computer networks occurs." In contrast to the coldness of the term 'cyberspace', the term 'the Internet', which came into common usage about the 1970s, came to represent the networking technologies that fostered communication between users and in so doing placed the importance of human users at its core. The important point in all this is to understand that cyberspace is much more than just the Internet; it is conceptually an artificial, virtual space that may or may not be connected to the wider Internet. For example, many industrial control systems that run Critical Nation Infrastructure are made up of networks of computers that are not connected to the Internet; however, this is still cyberspace. It's an interesting quirk of cyber culture that Gibson ultimately rejected the term cyberspace, commenting in 2000: "All I knew about the word 'cyberspace' when I coined it, was that it seemed like an effective buzzword. It seemed evocative and essentially meaningless. It was suggestive of something, but had no real semantic meaning, even for me...[4]"

With the amazing statistic that based on current trends, four out of five people globally will have a Facebook account by 2020, and with companies such as Google conducting research into using radical technologies such as weather

---

[2] Gibson, W. (1995). Burning Chrome. Harper Voyager; New Ed edition (27 Nov 1995)
[3] Gibson, W. (1995). Neuromancer. Harper voyager; New Ed Edition (27 Nov 1995)
[4] Neale, M. (2000). No Maps for These Territories. Documentary Distributed by Docurama
[5] Although purely paper-based OSINT is still very much in existence, and will always play a part within the investigative process, within this book the term 'OSINT' refers to purely cyberspace-based research activities.

balloons and aquatic buoys to spread Internet access to mountains and oceans, the importance of OSINT for investigators is only set to grow.

You probably picked up this book because you had become aware either from a colleague, conference, job advert or other source that OSINT was gaining prominence within the investigative community and you felt that you needed some kind of guide to get you up to speed with the current state of the art. Helping you on this journey is what this book is all about.

An effective OSINT capability is not simply a process list of things to do at certain points within an investigation, nor is it a 'black box' capability. It is in fact a combination of technical expertise, domain-specific knowledge and old-fashioned investigative smarts. As Richards J. Heuer, Jr, a giant in the intelligence analysis field, said, an effective intelligence capability is a blend of an art, craft and a science[6] and OSINT is no exception.

With regard to the approach that this work takes to the tools used for OSINT research, it's worth referencing another quotation from cyberpunk author William Gibson, who famously said "...the street finds its own uses for things[7]." This statement, which encapsulates the sentiment that users will find uses for technology that the original designers never envisaged, is a core theme that pervades this book's approach to the tools that can be applied to OSINT research. You will be introduced to tools designed primarily for salesmen, web

---

[6] Heur, R. (1999). Psychology of Intelligence Analysis. Center for the study of intelligence. Available from *www.cia.gov/library/center-for-the-study-of-intelligence/csi-publications/books-and-monographs/psychology-of-intelligence-analysis/*
[7] Gibson, W. (1995). Burning Chrome. Harper Voyager; New Ed edition (27 Nov 1995). Page 215

designers, computer hackers and the casual web user that although never intended for investigative use, have unique features that can be rallied to the investigator's cause.

The objective of this book is not to provide an exhaustive list of tools (Michael Bazzell's excellent work[8] does a far better job at that). Instead, it seeks to instruct you on a philosophical approach to effectively using OSINT within professional investigative work. Although tools and services are examined within the book (more than 30 in fact), they are only looked at to underline a higher-level investigative concept and to demonstrate the function of that specific class of tool. The reasoning behind this approach is that the OSINT toolbox is ever changing as old tools wither and die and new tools rise to replace them; however, the underlying principles (i.e. an understanding of the principles that underline a successful OSINT investigation) will equip the knowledgeable practitioner for years to come.

And on that note...

Four key concepts

This book is built around the following four foundations that underpin the entire field of OSINT as a professional practice:

1. *Multilayered* – there are three layers to the Internet: the Surface, Deep and Dark Web. They are commonly misunderstood; a working conceptualisation within the mind of the investigator is essential within effective

---

[8] Bazzell, M. (2014). Open Source Intelligence Techniques: Resources for Searching and Analyzing Online Information. CreateSpace Independent Publishing Platform; 3rd edition (1 Jan 2014)

OSINT professional practice. The beginnings of definitions of these terms are given below and are expanded upon through the remainder of this book.

a. *Surface Web* – is the part of the Internet that is accessible via mainstream web browsers such as Google or Bing. Typically, sites within this layer of the Internet are designed to be listed on mainstream search engines that are intended to be found easily by the casual web user. Much of the information on the Surface Web is common knowledge that is not sensitive.

b. *Deep Web* – is the part of the Internet that is not listed (or to use the more technical term, 'indexed') by the main search engines. The reason for this is that the technology used in Deep Web publishing platforms such as Facebook, Twitter and LinkedIn is not designed to be read and understood by the technology that drives searches engines such as Google. To be specific, Deep websites are not designed to be hidden by the publisher, it's just that the contents of Deep websites cannot be read by conventional search engines. Most of the information on the Surface Web has been placed there by the subject of the information via social media technologies such as Facebook. As such, a lot of the time most of the information that an investigator is seeking on an individual within the context of an investigation is located within the Deep Web; the main challenge for the investigator is getting access to this data.

c. *Dark Web* – is possibly the most mysterious and misreported of the three layers of the Internet. The Dark Web can only be accessed via the use of specialist pieces of anonymising software such as The

Onion Router (TOR). For the most part, websites and services placed onto the Dark Web are meant to be hidden from all but the most informed and technically savvy web user and often contain deeply criminal content (drugs, guns and child pornography are rife) vended on illicit online marketplaces. As it is the most overtly criminal section of the Internet, the Dark Web is a place only to go to if you have a specific remit to investigate crime within this space.

2. *Cyber geography* – just like physical geography, the Internet has its own unique 'regions' based upon linguistic divisions. For example, Russophone Internet users publish to the Internet in Russian and not English. Additionally, different linguistic groups publish different volumes of content to the Internet. As Anglophones have been connected to the Internet for the longest period, by far the dominating language (by volume) of the Internet is English. However, that is not to say that there are not many hundreds of thousands of pages published in other languages as well. Although this point may seem obvious with hindsight, cyber geography is a property of the Internet that is often overlooked by the novice and expert investigator alike. The impact of not fully appreciating this point is that if an investigator limits his or her search to just one linguistic sphere within one specific cyber geography then they are vastly diminishing their chance of success.

3. *Mixed medium* – at the layer of the user experience, the Internet (Surface, Deep or Dark) is not made up of one single technology. Instead, it is a complex mixture of searching and display technologies that all have their own unique set of rules that require specific techniques for the experienced investigator to penetrate.

Exhaustively enumerating all the different technologies and approaches required by the OSINT practitioner is not the objective of this book. What this book does seek to do is equip the investigator with the skills necessary to fully assess the risks and operational requirements needed to penetrate a new technological space on the Internet.

4. *Tangibility* – often the Internet is actively distinguished from 'the real world'. By using this term, it is implied that the Internet is somehow less tangible and hence less important to the human experience than events that occur within a physical space. Although this may have been the case 20 years ago, the Internet has become so deeply intertwined with our daily lives that for many users (particularly within Western economies) access to the Internet is as important as the provision of a stable electricity grid or clean water supply. Recent world events such as the Arab Spring and the ongoing unrest in Ukraine have demonstrated how integral the Internet has become to people's lives.

To credit myself with the observation of the preceding points would be wrong; instead, I merely advocated their centrality to OSINT as a professional practice.

What to expect from the rest of this book

The remainder of this book is built around the different tools and investigative approaches that are required when conducting research within the Surface, Deep and Dark Webs. Although there is more to OSINT than simply examining these three divisions of the Internet, this is an appropriate approach to OSINT due to the context that the focus on each web layer provides. This book will serve as more than merely a list of tools and instead facilitate the growth of an individual's ability to integrate OSINT into their existing investigative skill set. It is intended to be an explanation of theory via the demonstration of tools.

Although the value of the knowledge presented within the next chapters will vary depending upon the objective of the individual investigator, each concept should be examined in the order that they are presented. The professional engaged in due diligence will no doubt find the Deep Web chapter more immediately useful than the professional engaged in national security, but the threat landscape changes quickly and previously 'nice to know' knowledge quickly becomes the key to unlocking a future investigation[9]. Additionally, concepts are introduced early within this book and revisited in increasing detail through the remaining chapters.

---

[9] A prime example being how quickly Twitter aggregation tools, previously primarily only used for marketing, were quickly pressed into the service of nation security during the London riots of 2011.

CHAPTER 1: THE SURFACE WEB

The Surface Web is the most open and permissive of the three layers of cyberspace. Easily reachable via the most basic computer or mobile phone hardware, the Surface Web is something that almost everyone in the Western world and growing numbers in the developing world are becoming intimately familiar with. The Surface Web is the backbone for everyday business services such as email, web browsing, entertainment and commerce of all descriptions. With such a broad set of online resources available and the ease of access, the Surface Web is almost always the starting point of any OSINT project. Despite its ubiquity, the Surface Web does contain huge pools of data that are valuable to the investigator and often the central challenge to effectively using the Surface Web is locating the important pieces of information within the forest of irrelevant babble.

The core challenge of developing a practitioner's skill with regard to the Surface Web lies not in showing the usefulness of using this layer of cyberspace (that is innately obvious) but in highlighting to the investigator new possibilities for using the Surface Web.

Exercise: conduct a search

Before you continue further, conduct a short piece of research into the Nigerian terrorist group Boko Haram. Spend five minutes researching the group using the Internet in any way that you see fit.

Having run the preceding exercise several hundred times, I would hazard a guess that you did the following: used your computer's default web browser (Internet Explorer for

Windows, Safari for Mac users), used the Google of your home web domain (.co.uk, .ca, etc.) as your search engine, entered a couple of search phrases, read mostly articles from Wikipedia and mainstream news sites, and made no attempts to hide your identity while on the Internet.

Although these steps are all logical and where most OSINT investigations start, this is also where most OSINT investigations stop. Too often the OSINT part of an investigation is declared 'complete' after the preceding steps are taken. The remainder of this chapter is about expanding your investigative repertoire and imparting an understanding of *why* you need to do so.

 Consider for a moment...

Does the Internet look the same from every angle? In other words, are people in Russia looking at the same Internet as people in the UK? The answer to this point is explored in more depth later in this chapter in the *Cyber Geography* section.

Web browsers – the first steps

A web browser is the generic term for the class of software that is used in conjunction with a search engine to browse the Internet. The importance of web browsers as both a starting point for the practical section of this book and to OSINT professional practice in general, is that web browsers are the 'nuts and bolts' foundations that support the remainder of this book.

Typically, operating systems[10] such as the Microsoft Windows family and those loaded onto Macs come bundled

---

[10] An operating system is the piece of software that runs the hardware of your computer. In plain terms, it's the thing that you see on the screen when you boot up you computer.

with web browsers such as Internet Explorer and Safari. Although these web browsers are perfectly serviceable for the needs of an everyday web user, they are inadequate for the OSINT practitioner due to their lack of functionally and extendibility.

For the OSINT professional, having knowledge of just two non-standard web browsers can vastly expand investigative possibilities. This is due to the fact that certain pieces of software, called plugins, can be added to web browsers and make a huge difference to the insight that can be derived from a website as well as adding to the speed, efficiency and robustness of the results of an investigation.

Although new web browsers are coming onto the market almost every day, the author recommends to the reader that they use Google Chrome and Mozilla Firefox. Both products can be downloaded for free, and installing them involves a few clicks on the relevant pop-up boxes.

 Be warned!

Be very careful when installing any kind of software sourced from the Internet onto your computer as many apparently legitimate downloads are in fact just malicious malware delivery vehicles. If you are unsure how to differentiate legitimate from malicious software then consult your IT department or consult a knowledgeable colleague.

The reasons for choosing these two web browsers are as follows:

Flexibility

'Tabbed browsing' is the term used to describe the functionality within web browsers that allows multiple pages to be open within one web browsing window (or 'pane' to use the correct term). New sub-windows are opened by clicking on the areas shown in *Figure 1*.

Figure 1: Tabbed browsing in Chrome and Firefox

Although tabbed browsing is not unique to Firefox or Chrome, this functionality allows the investigator to have multiple windows open at any one time. This may seem a relatively trivial addition to an individual's OSINT skill set, but tabbed browsing is sometimes a departure from the way many older Internet users are accustomed to browsing the web. The benefit of mastering tabbed browsing across two separate web browsers is that multiple investigative threads can be followed and cross-referenced by the investigator at any one moment. In the highly visual environment of the Internet this approach can prove invaluable, especially if combined with a duel monitor display.

Extendibility with Add-Ons

Chrome and especially Firefox can have their functionality hugely extended by the addition of small pieces of software called add-ons.

Installing add-ons is easy: simply load the web browser you wish to install an add-on into, and then navigate to the online resource for that particular browser:

- *Chrome*: *https://chrome.google.com/webstore/category/ extensions*
- *Firefox: https://addons.mozilla.org/*

Once an appropriate online resource for the browser has loaded you can then add new add-ons directly from there[11].

There are thousands of available add-ons for both Firefox and Chrome and although most are irrelevant to OSINT professional practice, a few can make a difference within an investigation. As Firefox has been around far longer than Chrome, there are more useful add-ons for the OSINT practitioner for this platform. Some useful add-ons are listed next (all add-ons can be found by Googling the term 'Firefox add-on' plus the name of the add-on):

Table 1: Firefox plugins quick reference table

Tool	Function as described by provider	Where to find it once it's been installed into the Firefox browser	How to use it within an investigation
Unique Tools			
Flagfox[12]	Displays a country flag depicting the location of the current website's server and provides a multitude of tools such as site safety checks,	A little flag in the URL bar Domain Name: addons.mozilla.org IP Address: 63.245.216.132 Server Location: United States	Useful for quickly identifying which country a website is hosted in and the WHOIS information behind the site – very useful when dealing

---

[11] If further clarification of how to integrate add-ons into either Firefox or Chrome is required then judicious Googling will display many 'how to' instruction manuals on the subject. Additionally, the online video service YouTube lists several hundred videos discussing the subject with onscreen walkthroughs.

[12] *https://addons.mozilla.org/en-US/firefox/addon/flagfox/?src=search*

Tool	Function as described by provider	Where to find it once it's been installed into the Firefox browser	How to use it within an investigation
	WHOIS, translation, similar sites, validation, URL shortening and more		with constellations of fraudulent websites
Email Extractor[13]	Scrapes web page for any email addresses	Adds a small button next to the URL bar	Extremely useful for quickly extracting all email addresses from a web page. This tool will even extract emails from the computer code behind (and not visible to the user) a web page
Translate This![14]	Auto translate selected text	Right-click menu ("Translate This!" link)	Obvious
Map with Google Maps[15]	Auto maps selected addresses in Google Maps	Right-click menu	Useful for rapidly mapping addresses found in free-form text
Data Recovery Tools			
	What do you do when a page is	Shown in the following panel when encountering a broken website.	If a website goes offline,

---

[13] *https://addons.mozilla.org/en-US/firefox/addon/email-extractor/?src=search*
[14] *https://addons.mozilla.org/en-US/firefox/addon/translate-this/*
[15] *https://addons.mozilla.org/en-US/firefox/addon/directions-with-google-maps/?src=search*

Tool	Function as described by provider	Where to find it once it's been installed into the Firefox browser	How to use it within an investigation
Resurrect Pages[16]	dead but you still want to see it? Call in the clerics, and perform a resurrection	The options on the right (circled)	there are often multiple copies of that site on various Internet caches. This tool allows the user to investigate these caches to find these older records. Great if an original website is currently offline.
Memento Fox[17]	Time Travel for the Web. MementoFox implements the Memento protocol that links resources with their previous versions automatically, so you can see the web as it was in the past	Add a time slider directly under the URL bar	Allows the investigator to view what a website looked like in the past (if there is an archive record of course). Very useful for seeing how a website has developed over time and recovering incriminating facts that have been taken down by the user. Invaluable to fraud and liability investigators
Archiving and Preservation Tools			

[16] *https://addons.mozilla.org/en-US/firefox/addon/resurrect-pages/*
[17] *https://addons.mozilla.org/en-US/firefox/addon/mementofox/*

Tool	Function as described by provider	Where to find it once it's been installed into the Firefox browser	How to use it within an investigation
Easy Youtube Video Downloader Express[18]	Allows the download of YouTube videos in various formats	Appears as a button under a YouTube video	Used for archiving relevant YouTube videos to the user's home computer. As YouTube videos can be taken down at any time this is a great tool for preserving videos (note: this tool is not a forensic-grade video capture tool)
Abduction! – Webpage Screenshots Screen Capture[19]	Allows the user to take screenshots of a specific section of a web page	Right-click menu ("Save Page as Image…")	Preserve individual images or whole pages in a logical manner during an investigation (note: this tool is not a forensic-grade image capture tool)
Save text to File[20]	Save selected text to a txt file	Right-click menu ("Save Text to File")	Handy for making notes and memos as an investigation progresses
Image Search Tools			

---

[18] https://addons.mozilla.org/en-US/firefox/addon/easy-youtube-video-download/?src=search
[19] https://addons.mozilla.org/en-US/firefox/addon/abduction/
[20] https://addons.mozilla.org/en-US/firefox/addon/save-text-to-file/?src=search

1: The Surface Web

Tool	Function as described by provider	Where to find it once it's been installed into the Firefox browser	How to use it within an investigation
Search By Image in Google[21]	Access the Google image search	Right-click menu ("Search Google with this image")	Useful for finding related or similar images, i.e. more pictures of the same individual
TinEye Reverse Image Search	Access the TinEye image search (different from Google image search)	Right-click menu ("Search Image on TinEye")	Another image search tool, but different from the rest in that the service looks for exactly the same image reproduced on different sites across the Internet. Used to great effect by copyright-protection investigators to find examples of fake art
Meta Search Tool Add-ons			
Carrot2	Adds the search carrot meta search engine to the search engine selection menu[22]	Top-right search bar	Allows meta search engine use (looked at in more detail in the next section) direct from the Firefox browser

One point of caution to make regarding add-ons is that the

---

[21] https://addons.mozilla.org/en-US/firefox/addon/search-by-image-by-google/
[22] https://addons.mozilla.org/en-US/firefox/addon/carrot2/?src=userprofile

19

more that are added to a web browser, the slower the browser will run. With a handful of add-ons the slowdown in browser performance is negligible; however, with ten or more add-ons running the debilitating effects on browser speed become obvious. The solution to this issue is to toggle individual add-ons on and off depending on the needs of the investigator. This can be done via the "Tools – Add-ons" menu that brings up the control panel shown in *Figure 2* in the Firefox browser.

Figure 2: Extension (add-ons) control panel in Firefox

Clicking the Disable button will temporarily remove that add-on from the system-processing load of the Firefox browser. Obviously the add-on can be easily reactivated by clicking the *Enable* button when the user wishes to use that specific software tool again.

By their very nature add-ons are not mainstream pieces of software. Lone, mostly unpaid software developers are often the authors and many have limited time and resources to support their products. This means that add-ons periodically break, as web technologies change and add-ons become outdated as the developers fail to keep pace with these new developments. As such, close management of these pieces of software (installing updates, removing hopelessly broken add-ons) is just an unfortunate part of using add-ons. However, the benefit of add-ons outweighs the management overhead.

Speed

If Google's Chrome browser excels at one thing, it's speed. Chrome has been designed for the modern generation of Internet users who grew up being weaned on broadband Internet connections with the expectation of lightning-fast page loading[23]. Although increasing Internet speeds may have led to an overall decline in attention spans, the benefits of rapid page loading that Chrome provides to the OSINT practitioner are undeniable.

Additionally, Chrome has an extremely useful way of visualising text searches within a specific web page, a function activated by holding down Ctrl+F in Windows and Cmd+F on a Mac and then entering the desired search phrase (results shown in *Figure 3*).

Figure 3: Search result flags in Chrome (circled)

---

[23] I remember during the era of dial-up modems when I could make a cup of coffee while a page loaded – happy days…

This is particularly useful for interrogating web pages for specific search terms that can often prove elusive within reams of text. This feature of Chrome can be a huge time-saver in a situation where it is not obvious how a web page is related to a search term. By using the search, the investigator can quickly locate where a term such as a name, phone number or email address occurs within a body of text, which allows the investigator to rapidly contextualise the data presented within the page and decide if that particular page is relevant to the investigation or not.

 Chapter key learning point: investigate outside the box

The core message that this chapter communicates is that the skilled OSINT investigator should break away from the constraints of viewing one web page within one web browser. Although you will almost certainly use the Internet for personal reasons, using the Internet for professional purposes demands a different approach. By using the technologies and approaches outlined within this chapter, you can agilely pivot through an informational space as new investigative opportunities present themselves.

Combining Chrome's tabbed browsing, fast loading speed and visual search capabilities, the web browser allows the skilled OSINT practitioner to almost concurrently examine hundreds of web pages at speed, discarding the irrelevant and archiving the useful as the search progresses.

Search engines

Recall the exercise at the start of this chapter and the Author's criticism of the exclusive use of Google as a tool for OSINT research. The reader may wonder where the Author's opinion on this issue may come from. Try the next exercise before we explore this point further:

✎ ***Exercise: spot the difference***

Open a web browser (either Firefox or Chrome) and conduct an image search[24] for the individual 'Stewart Bertram' in Google, Yahoo and Bing and place the results next to one another using tabbed browsing. Then spot the difference between the results presented by each browser.

The result that you will no doubt be viewing after completing the exercise is three pages of images. Although many of the results are identical across the three web browsers, as you scroll down that page of each of the three results pages you will see that there is an increasing divergence between the images that the three search engines have produced and large numbers of images that are unique to specific search engines.

The image results vary between the search engines due to the fact that each search engine is drawing from different sources of data when presenting its results.

 Side knowledge: search engine indexing

Have you ever wondered how search engines generate their results? A large part of the process involves software agents autonomously surfing the Internet and trying to understand what the core themes of a particular website are. This process is called indexing and allows search engines such as Google to match search strings from a user to relevant web pages. Each search engine uses different indexing algorithms; as such, the same search yields different results when used across a number of search engines. The power of search engines and the indexes they create is that without them users would have to know the exact address (or Uniform Resource Locator (URL)) to visit a site. The true power of an index is that it allows search engines to match human search terms such as 'shopping in London' to an appropriate list of websites for that search term.

The obvious question to ask is how different are search results across the main search engine providers? According to a joint study carried out by the search engine provider Dogpile,

---

[24] The image search button is located just beneath the search bar in Google.

Queensland University of Technology and the Pennsylvania State University, nearly a whopping 90 percent[25] of search results were unique to one of the four major search engine providers. Based on these stats and the tangible proof provided by the 'Spot the difference' exercise, it's the author's hope that the reader understands why the author advocates using more than one search engine to conduct OSINT. In plain terms: if you are doing OSINT research using just Google and are not finding the result that you are looking for, you are only examining a tiny proportion of the available sources.

 Key learning point: Google is not the Internet

Contrary to popular belief, the index of Google does not contain the address of every Internet site on the web. In fact no one really knows how many websites are actually on the Internet. Although Google's database is huge (possible the largest database on Earth), within the infinite space that is the Internet even this database may in fact be tiny.

Search engines such as Google and Bing can be described as 'single-source intelligence' and using single sources of intelligence within the context of an investigation is generally considered to be a bad thing by professionals.

So if that is the problem, what is the solution? Enter meta search engines...

Search engines – meta search engines

Simply put, meta search engines are search engines that query other search engines and aggregate these search results. Take a few moments to review the list of meta search engines shown next; they can be reached by

---

[25] Sol. (9 Dec 2008). Dogpile comes out at the top of the pile. Download from *http://federatedsearchblog.com/2007/12/09/dogpile-comes-out-at-the-top-of-the-pile/*

Googling the name, or alternatively a link is provided to the service as a footnote.

Table 2: Meta search engine quick reference table

Meta Search Engine	Source Search Engines	Unique Features
Early-stage Investigative Tools		
ZUULA [26]	Google, Yahoo, Bing	Queries the largest number of single-source search engines and presents them using tabbed browsing. Also provides a useful 'breadcrumb' display of previously used search strings
dögpile [27]	Google, Yahoo	Nothing special, apart from being a fast tool for a meta browser
PolyMeta [28]	Google, Yahoo, Bing, Ask	Very useful concept mapping feature (Windows only)
Mid- to Late-stage Investigative Tools		
iSEEK Targeted Discovery [29]	Unknown – developer does not reveal this information	Excellent entity extraction and tag clouding functionality
Cluuz. [30]	Unknown – developer does not reveal this information	Entity relationship map
Carrot2 Clustering Engine [31]	Google, Bing	Unique approach to visualising tag clouds of search results

---

[26] www.zuula.com
[27] www.dogpile.com
[28] www.polymeta.com
[29] www.iseek.com
[30] www.cluuz.com
[31] http://search.carrot2.org/stable/search

Although the preceding list may prove interesting to the busy investigator, the list is in effect the digital equivalent of a 'flash of a stocking top' and is unlikely to fully demonstrate the benefits of these tools to OSINT professional practice. The following points step beyond a superficial presentation of the features of the tools by delving deeper into the benefits each can bring to an investigation:

- *Throwing a wide net*: for the OSINT practitioner the most basic benefit of meta search engines over single-source tools is to throw the widest possible investigative net to trawl the web for data of interest. The Dogpile tool is a meta search engine that queries Google and Bing to obtain its result[32], and is a viable replacement for the default Google tool used during the casual searching that occurs at the start of any OSINT project. Zuula is similar to the 'no frills' Dogpile but differs in that it queries nine separate search engines for its results[33]. Zuula also provides a 'Recent Search' function that saves a user's previous searches to a left-aligned toolbar. This can prove handy when exploring a large field of search results as the investigator is free to explore multiple angles within the data, safe in the knowledge that they can easily return to a more relevant search term at any point. The investigator should consider Dogpile as a 'day-to-day' search engine and Zuula as a tool to use when an investigation has run completely dry.

- *Concept mapping*: taking a step back from a straight explanation of tools and technique, it's worth

---

[32] Dogpile has queried Bing in the past and may do so again in the future.
[33] As of writing this book, many of the search engine connections to Zuula are broken. The site experiences periodic outages and the status of the development for this project is unknown.

considering what a website is actually trying to do. Every website is, at its core, trying to communicate information to the reader. Whereas conventional search engines tend to just represent a description of what information is contained within a site, some meta search engines have software tools that attempt to present the core themes of the site to the user. Polymeta is a search engine with its unique 'Concept Map' feature (available on Windows operating systems only, with up-to-date Java settings). The benefit of using a concept map within an OSINT task is that the investigator is presented with a conceptual map of the subject they are researching. Not only does this generate new investigative leads but also allows the user to assimilate new data and visualise the cornerstones of an investigation much quicker than when limiting oneself to single-source search engines.

The previous theory points and preceding tools are ideal for the start of an OSINT project when the investigator's effort is focused on 'picking up the scent' and conceptualising the key issue surrounding a case. Of course all cases develop in time and the initial rapid sense-making efforts give way to a more measured approach to an investigation, as the need for precise details becomes apparent. The following meta search tools are particularly useful once an investigation has reached this stage:

 Side knowledge: accuracy of Entity Extraction tools

You may notice a few odd entries are included in the Entity Extraction list within iSeek, e.g. places within people categories and so on. These small errors should in no way discredit the tool. Entity Extraction is a subfield of artificial intelligence and is an extremely difficult process to implement, especially in the lightning-fast speed of web browsing. As such, minor errors are to be expected and accepted by the OSINT practitioner.

Granular refinement of investigative details: iSeek is very useful within the later stages of an investigation due to the powerful Entity Extraction engine integrated into the software. Entity Extraction is a process by which a computer program examines a body of text within a document set, finds the main themes and then creates bookmarks across the document set according to defined categories such as date, place, person and so on. The result of this is that the user can easily filter the document according to the data within the categories that the software extracts, e.g. Stewart Bertram (category: people), Canada (category: countries). This in itself is a useful feature for an investigator. However, the really clever part of the iSeek Entity Extraction process is that there is not a predefined list of items that the tool works from when placing document text within each category. Entity Extraction works by identifying significant elements within the text and then examining the context in which they are used, to determine the appropriate categorisation. As an example of how this process works, take the two phrases "the jaguar eats meat" and "the Jaguar eats gas." In both cases the categorisation of the Jaguar as either an animal or car comes from the context provided by the remainder of the sentence. The power of iSeek's Entity Extraction tool to the investigator is that it provides a huge amount of granular facts along with a map of how they fit together, which can be used to great effect by the skilled investigator to advance any OSINT project.

Boko Haram

As a demonstration of this technique try running Boko Haram through iSeek and then combining the results from different categories (i.e. the phrase Boko Haram with a place and a date), within a Google search. Do you feel this approach yields any better (i.e. more insightful and precise) results than a straight Google search?

Continuing the theme of granularity, Cluuz is another unique meta search engine that is worthy of inclusion within the OSINT practitioner's toolbox. What separates Cluuz from the rest of the meta search engine pack is the integrated tools that allow the software to not only conduct Entity Extraction but also to visualise how these entities map together (example shown in *Figure 4*).

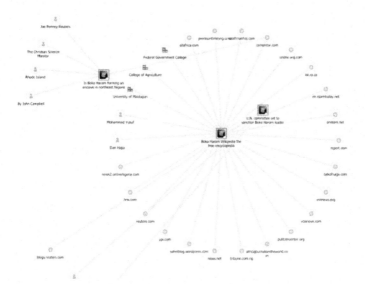

Figure 4: Cluuz network diagram

A visualisation such as the preceding one is created by clicking on the small network diagram that is placed next to the search result in the main window.

The Cluuz tool can be particularly useful when the investigator has a clear idea of a website or well-defined entity (the exact spelling of the name of a person of interest, company name and so on) that is linked to a case. Focusing the Cluuz tool on a specific website and then exploring the data using the social network graphs that the software generates, can clarify facts and clearly identify the sources of data where the case information is coming from. Additionally, the results that Cluuz presents to the investigator, if used correctly, are excellent at separating data on a specific individual from the mass of generic data that has been generated by a search on a common name (this technique is explored in more detail in *Chapter 2: Deep Web*).

Returning to the immediate usefulness of Cluuz, the tool can be very useful during the initial phases of an investigation that has an individual website as the starting point. Clicking on the Advanced tab reveals two new search boxes; the box labelled *Site(s)?* allows the user to input the address of a specific website (shown in *Figure 5*).

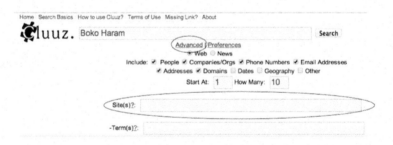

Figure 5: Site search revealed by clicking on the Advanced tab

When the search is run a network diagram is generated for the specific site entered into the *Site(s)?* box. This can prove incredibly useful in increasing the velocity of the initial stages of an investigation.

In conclusion, the main focus of the early-stage tools is to expand the search area of an investigation as wide as possible. Effectively using the mid- to late-stage tools requires the investigator to actually pay closer attention to the outputs of the analytical tools integrated into the search engines (iSeek's Entity Extraction list and Cluuz's social network graphs) than the search results that the engines return. This concept is usually a change in approach to OSINT for many investigators new and old alike. However, at this point quoting the classic saying, *"don't look at your finger, look at the moon"* becomes appropriate. The user's finger is an obvious analogy to a list of search results, and the moon is the equivalent of the enhanced understanding that meta search tools can provide

---

 Top tip: images and meta search engines

All the meta search engines are extremely poor at image searching and it would appear that most simply pull from the Google image search results. When looking for specific images, say of a person, investigators should go individually to the 'big three' search engines (Google, Yahoo and Bing) and view image search results separately within each search engine.

You might have noticed that we have not covered the Carrot2 Cluster search engine yet, partly because the author wants to save the best for last and partly because it fits particularly well with the next theoretical section.

Cyber geography

One of the four key points outlined in the introduction was the concept of cyber geography. The author would posit that this idea is a crucial theoretical concept that any skilled OSINT practitioner needs to master.

To illustrate the effect and importance of cyber geography, examine the two images show next in *Figure 6*:

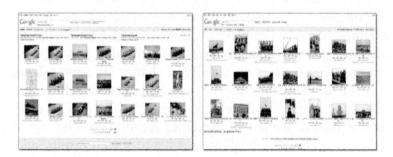

Figure 6: Cyber Geography in action

Both images are screenshots of the results of a Google image search for the phrase 'Tiananmen Square' that were taken on the twenty-fifth anniversary of the massacre that occurred in the square in 1989[34]. The one on the left shows the results of the search conducted via Google.co.uk, and the one on the right shows the results of the same search conducted using Google.cn (the Chinese-specific Google). The obvious difference between the two results pages is possibly the sharpest demonstration of how cyber geography affects the search results the user sees. For the 'on the ground' OSINT practitioner the practical effect of cyber geography is that an investigator can miss huge volumes of relevant data if he is looking in the wrong Internet region.

A more granular explanation of why cyber geography so drastically affects the results that search engines generate comes from how the structure of the Internet is designed and how search engines are used by mainstream users.

---

[34] If you are interested in seeing exactly which websites are censored in which countries, take a look at *Herdict.org*, a site that tracks Internet censorship.

In the early days of the Internet, or ARPANET as it was called then, all website addresses were compiled into a central list and periodically distributed to all network hosts. As the Internet grew this system quickly became unwieldy and a number of technical solutions were developed to make the rapidly expanding Internet more user friendly. The Domain Name System (more commonly, DNS) became the equivalent of a phone book for the Internet that translated machine-readable address, called Internet Protocol addresses, into human-readable addresses, e.g. *www.microsoft.com* (human readable), 134.170.184.133 (machine-readable IP address). An essential component of the DNS system is the subcategories called Top Level Domains (TLDs), which always show in a human-readable web address as the final part of the text, i.e. .com, .co.uk and so on. The most obvious way of categorising TLDs within the DNS records was to allocate one TLD to each country, which created the current cyber geography that we know today. To expand their user base to people in as many countries as possible, search engine providers were quick to develop specialist indexes and search interfaces for each TLD, e.g. Google.ca is a specialist index for the Canadian TLD space.

 Side knowledge: 'the Internet' is not a single entity

The term 'Internet' implies that the Internet is one single technology, being administrated by a centralised command and control body. An important thing to understand for the OSINT practitioner is that the Internet is in fact a conglomerate of many technologies and that the DNS system and the various search engines are in fact two separate technologies. The critical point of this piece of knowledge is that just because a search engine index does not have a record of a website does not mean that it does not exist. Indeed it is possible that the majority of the Internet is not listed on any search engine at all.

Of course how people use search engines fundamentally affects how they are designed and research has shown that about 50% of searches on Google are for information about services that are in the same geographic location as the user. Search engine results are ordered according to the physical geography of the user, e.g. a London-based user searching for 'Curry restaurants' will be shown London-based results first with results on Mumbai-based restaurants being many pages back in the search results. As the majority of search engine providers generate their income via advertising, and as the majority of users select search engines based on the relevance of the results, it is obvious why companies such as Google and Yahoo structure their indexing process so heavily around physical geography. Although for the everyday user this situation is fine, the effects of cyber geography can severely constrain an investigator.

Although the theory behind cyber geography is involved, thankfully the solution to the issue is relatively simple. Due to the fact that many of the main search providers have created engines specifically configured for various geographic regions, it's merely a case of finding the appropriate search engine for that region via a search within the provider's main .com site, e.g. a search in Google.com for the phrase 'Google Canada' returns Google.**ca**, the Google engine specifically designed for the Canadian market.

 Top tip: No Country Redirect

When conducting searches across multiple cyber geographies, Google has an annoying tendency to return users back to their 'home' domain after a few searches. This can be extremely frustrating if one is engaged in an intensive regional-specific OSINT project. The way around this issue is the No Country Redirect command, by typing the characters /NCR into the URL bar in the web browser and pressing enter, e.g. Google.ca/NCR. This simple command then locks that pane of a browser to the selected search engine.

There are of course 196 countries (counting Taiwan) in the world, with a still greater number of TLDs not allocated to a country (.aq is the domain for Antarctica!). All of these TLDs have potentially useful dates on a research subject within them and this complex cyber topography gives rise to the obvious question of 'which TLD should an OSINT practitioner start an investigation in?' This question dovetails nicely with the functionality of the Carrot2 meta search engine.

The designers of Carrot2 describe it as a 'clustering engine,' by which they are implying it attempts to present to the user an easily readable, aggregated view of the data within a search. Activating the clustering feature of Carrot2 is done by clicking on the Circles and FoamTree tabs within the browser (shown in *Figure 7*):

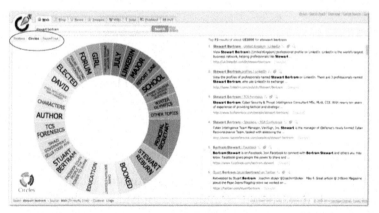

Figure 7: Folders, Circles and FoamTree tabs in Carrot2 (Circles selected)

The way to interpret the slightly hallucinogenic output of Carrot2 shown in Figure 7, is to use each of the coloured segments to navigate the associated document sets. At this point take a moment to review the various categories, i.e. people, places and so on of data presented by the wheel in *Figure 7*. Which is the most useful category of data presented with this search?

I believe the most useful category of data that Carrot2 presents is geographic associated with a search topic, as this gives the shrewd investigator a clear direction on which TLD they should look within in relation to a search. Taking this overt focus on cyber geography a step further, Carrot2 can be easily configured to display websites clustered by TLD. This feature is activated by clicking FoamTree, More Options and then selecting in the Cluster with the drop-down box the 'By URL' option. When properly configured this generates results similar to *Figure 8*:

Figure 8: Cluster by URL results in a Carrot2 search

This result is most useful to the investigator when focusing on the TLDs shown around the outside of the display. These results represent the hidden nooks of the Internet, and often hold within them data that would be overlooked by mainstream search engines due to their proclivity to concentrate on the .org and .com domains. Combining Carrot2's ability to highlight important TLDs with a good foreign language search engine can quickly advance any OSINT task that spans multiple geographies and linguistic spheres.

Cyber geography is one of the simplest but often overlooked features of OSINT tradecraft. With hindsight, when the theoretical foundations and practical workarounds are explained, cyber geography seems obvious; but more than any other point examined within this book, cyber geography pervades almost every aspect of OSINT professional practice. Ignore it at your peril…

(Slightly below) the Surface Web

So far this chapter has concentrated on harvesting data in ways that the average web user will be relatively familiar with. However, there is a huge pool of data that sits slightly beneath the websites and the files that can only be accessed with specialist knowledge and tools. This section examines some of these tools used to pull back the covers of data held on the Surface Web.

Metadata (subsurface data)

Metadata is data that describes other types of data. For example, the .docx file extension tells a computer's operating system that the file is a Word document and should be opened within the Microsoft Office program. Although each individual file contains many hundreds and even thousands of points of metadata, certain fields are more useful to the investigator than others. The three most important metadata fields to be aware of are:

1. *File creation date*: this is typically interpreted as the date when the file was originally created by the user. Be warned! The date can be tampered with and inadvertently altered by both the user and the actions of services on the computer system such as antivirus

programs. As such, the file creation date should only be used as intelligence to advance an investigation as opposed to being hard evidence[35]. Having said that, this piece of metadata can be very useful in constructing a timeline of events by mapping file content within the creation date within the metadata.

2. *File author*: typically, the username used to log in to the operating system of the computer that initially created the file is recorded within the meta of that file. This can prove insightful if the username reflects the name of the person whose login created the file.

3. *Latitude and longitude where the file was created (for image files only)*: most modern camera devices, including phones and tablets, will typically have some kind of GPS system built in. The latitude and longitude where a photograph was taken is stamped into the metadata of the image. Clearly this can be of huge benefit to an investigation and has proven so in extreme cases involving kidnap and ransom. One point to note is that not all images have this metadata within them, particularly if the image has been uploaded to a social media platform, which usually deliberately strips metadata from uploaded files.

Although the preceding metadata only gives three points of information on a file, if the investigator has the ability to get creative with this data then there are a number of ways that these data points can be effectively used. For example, file creation dates can be used to challenge witness testimony within an interview context, and location information attached to images can tangibly link events to locations.

---

[35] Computer forensic technique that can be used to enter the file creation date and other dates associated within files into an evidence chain. However, this is a highly specialist skill that is outside the scope of this book.

Extracting metadata from a digital artifact is surprisingly easy, with the creation date and author information being available by right-clicking on a file icon and then clicking on the Properties option. The latitude and longitude within the images is slightly more difficult to extract and requires specialist software to do so. Luckily this software is freely available online from resources such as *http://regex.info/exif.cgi*.

FOCA search tools

FOCA is an exceptionally powerful desktop search tool that leverages the advanced search syntax of Google, Yahoo and Bing to 'scrape' a target website for a huge range of file types. The program works by enumerating a website and searching for file paths to documents. Once it has identified these docs the user is free to download these files to their own machine. The power of FOCA lies in a number of areas: firstly, it rapidly automates the reparative task of entering complex search syntax for each file type into the three search engines FOCA utilises. Secondly, it assists in the mass extraction of metadata from the reports that it recovers. Thirdly and most importantly, FOCA has the ability to recover documents from a website that have no explicit download links on the site's pages. This almost magical ability, combined within the program's other functions, creates a powerful tool for the investigator that can rapidly increase the scale, scope and speed of an investigation. As of writing this book, FOCA is freely available from downloadcrew.co.uk/article/22211-foca_free.

Specialist search syntax

The majority of, if not all, search engines let users specify specialist syntax to generate unique results. The incentive for the investigator to use specialist syntax is that by effectively doing so, unique and insightful results can be gained that would not otherwise be revealed by merely entering search terms into a search engine.

The basic foundation for all search syntax is the AND, OR and NOT principles borrowed from a branch of discrete mathematics called Set Theory. These three basic operators are the basis upon which search engine algorithm results return data:

1. *AND* – returns results that contains all elements of the submitted search terms, e.g. the search *Fish Chips* would only return pages that contained both Fish and Chips (note: there is no need to explicitly specify the AND operator to most search engines as this is used by default within search strings. Additionally, search engines extract conjunctions such as *and, but* and *then* from search results as they are far too common in language to effectively match a search to a result).

2. *OR* – returns results that contain either elements of the search terms, e.g. *Fish OR Chips* would return pages that solely mentioned the distinct concepts of Fish or Chips as well as pages that mentioned both (note: the OR operator must be explicitly entered into the search engine with a capitalised *OR* between search terms).

3. *NOT* – one of the more strange mathematical concepts, NOT specifies a concept that should not be included in a set of search results. For example, *Fish NOT Chips* would return pages that contained the *Fish* concept with no mention of the *Chips* concept (note: NOT is specified by the – sign, so *Fish NOT Chips* would be entered into Google as *Fish –Chips*).

Although AND is used by default, OR and NOT can provide significant benefits during an investigation. OR throws the investigative net as wide as possible and NOT can be useful in removing concepts that are dominating a search result group and potentially obscuring useful data, e.g. *Employees Microsoft –'Bill Gates'* would show you who worked for Microsoft free from the company's most famous employee.

AND, OR and NOT are the most basic specialist search syntax. However, they effectively introduce the concept of search syntax and what can be achieved with these techniques.

There are a number of books that are devoted solely to search syntax, or 'Google Kung-Fu' to use the correct computer hacker terminology. The author recommends the reader read *Google Hacking*[36], which despite being nearly eight years old is still an excellent starting point to this niche of OSINT research. The author would also like to highlight a number of specialist search syntax strings and place them within the context of OSINT that the rest of this book focuses on. Listed below are five examples of specialist search syntax that, although not commonly known, are vital to building a more effective OSINT toolkit for the individual investigator.

 **AND as default**

It often surprises investigators that the default setting for almost all search engines is the AND operator. The result of this is that if the investigator insists on simply submitting text as a search string with no additional syntax the returned results will be extremely limited. Combining this approach with simply using Google as the main source of information further reduces the chances of success for the investigator.

Table 3: Key specialist search syntax

Search Syntax (search syntax in italics, input data in bold)	Search Engine	Explanation
ip: **xx.xxx.xxx.x**	Bing (unique)	List all websites hosted on an IP address. Very useful as this can show site importance not listed on any search engine index
site: **www.asite.com/**	Bing (unique)	List all pages on a specific website. Great for making sure that you have examined all pages on a site of interest
Search term *domain:* **www.asite.com/**	Bing but similar functionality in other search engines	Look for something specific within a defined website
"search term"	Google but similar functionality in other search engines	Prevent the spelling corrector from automatically correcting searches. Useful for unusual searches
Search term*: image*	Yahoo (unique)	Return pages with the search term in an image. Good for advanced people stalking

---

[36] Long, J. Temmingh, R. Petkov, P. (2007). Google Hacking. Syngress

One point to note about these searches is that many of them only work in a specific search engine, which continues the earlier theme that there is no one perfect solution for OSINT and that a blend of tools is necessary to achieve maximum effect.

Specialist web investigation tools

Most OSINT tools are similar to the FOCA tools discussed earlier in that although they allow faster access to data, they do not in themselves give access to any more data than if the investigator conducted a search or action manually. The following three OSINT tools buck this trend and give access to unique data that can be critical in advancing an investigation:

1. *DomainTools*: whenever a website is hosted on a Surface Web Internet server the designer is required to provide a set of details including contact name, email address, telephone number and physical address of the owner of the site. This data is collectively known as WHOIS data and is publicly available (surprisingly) via services such as DomainTools. In addition to a straight WHOIS lookup, DomainTools can provide a host of other services that can prove useful for the investigator:
   a. *Reverse WHOIS lookup* – find all sites that have commonalities within the WHOIS registration data. As designers tend to reuse registration details, this is an incredible tool for expanding the scope of an investigation as it finds links between otherwise disparate websites.
   b. *DomainTools monitors* – tracks activity on specific domains, e.g. changes in WHOIS and so on, which is useful for tracking changes in large constellations of suspicious sites.

c. *Screenshots* – see how a site used to be in the past.

d. *Reverse MX* – somewhat more technical but in essence websites are often configured to share an email service. The MX record provides access for multiple domains to the same email server and is another way to link suspicions domains.

2. *web.archive.org*: within this site is hosted the Wayback Machine (WBM), a tool that gives access to web.archive.org's historical record of the Internet. This incredible project seeks to archive as much of the Internet as possible and pieces of autonomous software called spider run constantly collect images of websites on behalf of web.archive.org. The archive goes back to 2005 and users are free to browse these sites via the WBM interface. One point to note is that all websites stored within web.archive.org are no longer hosted on the original web spaces that they were designed for; as such, any WHOIS searches via DomainTools will return registration information for web.archive.org and not the original site. Despite this the WBM is an incredibly useful tool for viewing how sites have developed over time and as the sites are stored on web.archive.org's servers (and hence effectively out of the control of the original authors) any incriminating information is stored for posterity within the archive as well.

3. *Google Earth*: often overlooked as just another tool, Google Earth and the imagery it contains can provide critical insight on a location if used correctly. Telltale indicators such as children's toys and types of industrial equipment can provide key indicators with regard to the use of a geographic location and its occupants. One point to note is that Google Earth is not a real-time monitoring tool and the imagery within the service is dated.

How dated can be seen by the small date/time information displayed in each Google Earth image that indicates when the image was originally created.

Suggested search and the knowledge of the crowd

Have you noticed when using Google that when you type in the start of a search term Google makes suggestions via a drop-down box of what it thinks you might be searching for?

Figure 9: Google suggested search example

This is called 'suggested search' and is one of the most useful features of Google and other search engines. Of course the Google algorithm, just like all other computational constructs, has no idea what you mean when you type in a search term; however, it does know that other users have searched for similar things that bear a relation to the initial part of your search string. For example, Google suggests 'James Bond' when a user types in 'James' as 'Bond' is the most commonly associated term for 'James'.

This effect is created by Google data mining hundreds of thousands of search terms to identify relations between search terms. This is in effect pattern matching on a grand scale and this neat technical trick taps into what sociologists have called the 'knowledge of the crowd'. As well as being an impressive technical party trick, suggested search can be useful for researchers due to its ability to highlight entities important to a case that the investigator might not have come across as part of their own investigation.

 The right to be forgotten

Having one's name associated with undesirable entities and concepts such as 'fraudster' is not a happy situation to be in and can seriously damage an individual's standing in today's information society. Negative association has become such a serious issue that many individuals have taken legal action against service providers such as Google to remove negative suggested search results[37]. People legally challenging suggested search results is part of a wider developing concept called the 'right to be forgotten', which at its core proposes that an individual should have the right to remove personal information from the Internet as they age.

Take, for example, the search phrase 'Boko Haram'. Common suggested searches that Google returns include generic phrases such as 'terrorist' and 'atrocity'; however, there are often terms suggested such as 'Maiduguri', the town in northern Nigeria that the group's geographic centre of gravity revolves around. The important point is that although the researcher may not have known that Maiduguri was associated with Boko Haram, others did, and they searched for articles using both entities. By querying the suggested search database in Google the investigator has the ability to vastly speed up their investigation by tapping into the knowledge that has been generated by others.

---

[37] *https://reportingproject.net/occrp/index.php/en/ccwatch/cc-watch-briefs/2571-hong-kong-man-sues-google-over-search-suggestions*

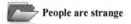 **People are strange**

Records within the suggested search database are not created by a few casual searches; instead, many thousands of repetitions of a search phrase are required to create a suggested search. The majority of these suggestions make complete sense; however, some of them are decidedly strange. Try entering the phrase *'sometimes I like to lie'* and see what comes back. Thousands of people have entered the result as a search term for this strange suggested search to be created...

As with just about everything within this book there is a specialist tool for querying the suggested search database in Google: *http://soovle.com/*.

Soovle has the added benefit of searching the Wikipedia, Amazon, Yahoo, Bing, YouTube and Answers suggested search datasets as well.

Conclusion

The Surface Web is the most easily accessible and permissive layer of the Internet and will most likely be where the majority of researchers spend the majority of their time. The Surface Web also provides the most variety for the application of novel tools and techniques, hence the length of this chapter compared to the following chapters in this book.

CHAPTER 2: DEEP WEB

Compared to the Surface Web and the Dark Web, the Deep Web is the most topographically complex of the three cyber domains, both in terms of the technology used to create the Deep Web and the way people use it. Although easily accessible with the web browsing software that is used to access the Surface Web, finding the valuable information that is locked within the Deep Web is more of an art than the science of Surface Web mining. A good way to conceptualise the investigative approach to the Deep Web is that information within this layer of cyberspace that is relevant to an investigation is not hidden; it's just slightly out of sight.

Successfully mining the Deep Web can provide the most immediate gains in terms of an increased volume of raw data. This data can prove valuable for the OSINT investigator involved in any work that deals with people or groups as the focus of the investigation. To borrow from a law enforcement term, OSINT investigation within the Deep Web layer of the Internet typically has a focus on a 'person of interest,' a generic term for an individual who may become a suspect or is somehow closely linked to an investigation. The remainder of this chapter carries forward this concept, with the objective of equipping the investigation with enhanced tools to mine the Deep Web.

The Deep Web and social media technology

If there is one web technology that has driven the growth of the Deep Web it is social media technology. Platforms such as the two giants, Facebook and Twitter, turned practices such as 'tweeting'[38], 'trolling'[39], 'spamming'[40], and 'flaming'[41] into global pastimes. The author cannot overstate the importance of social media to the growth of the Deep Web; Facebook alone reached more than one billion users by about 2013[42]. With the current world population assessed at about seven billion, Facebook user rates mean that incredibly more than one-sixth of the entire world population has a Facebook account. This unprecedented representation of the global human population has been facilitated largely by the flexibility of the technology that social media is constructed from. With the number of Internet users predicted to reach more than five billion by 2020[43], the importance of social media to OSINT professional practice will only grow.

> *The difference between social media technology and social media platforms*
>
> A social media platform is the term used for a specific social media service provider, e.g. Facebook, LinkedIn, Bebo and so on. Social media technology is a generic term used to encapsulate all the different platforms that are currently contributing to the huge growth of the 'social web', i.e. the web content on the Internet being generated solely on social media platforms.

Social media technology is built to grow on a huge scale, with Facebook and similar providers building vast server farms to hold the millions of new profiles created by users,

---

[38] When a user posts a message on the Twitter platform.
[39] Deliberately posting provocative messages to lure new users to a forum into posting
[40] Flooding a user or forum with a deluge of messages.
[41] Deluge of aggressive messages.
[42] http://thenextweb.com/facebook/2014/01/29/facebook-passes-1-23-billion-monthly-active-users-945-million-mobile-users-757-million-daily-users/.
[43] www.networkworld.com/article/2238913/wireless/10-fool-proof-predictions-for-the-internet-in-2020.html.

who require no programming skills to design and deploy a website. Given the fact that social media is virtually unregulated, it is obvious that the Deep Web can prove to be a treasure trove for the skilled investigator.

Who watches the watchers?

Fact: did you know that if you collected together all the employees of Facebook, Twitter and LinkedIn, past and present, they would comfortably fit into Madison Square Garden? This fact is surprising given that these three services collectively hold accounts and personal data of over one-fifth of the entire world population. Given the disparity in the number of service users compared to the number of service providers, it becomes obvious that there is no way that service providers like Facebook can track the content of each post and profile on their platform. This explains the sometimes illegal and extreme content of many social media platforms.

A standard rule is that all content posted to any social media platform is uniquely attributable to an individual account, and almost all social media accounts track back to one identifiable individual. Taking this point into account, and the fact that social media is virtually unregulated, if used effectively then information derived from social media (SOCMINT, to borrow an acronym from Sir David Omand[44] *et al*) can provide a direct feed of primary source information to the skilled investigator.

Although investigation within the social media web space may be a relatively new practice, attempting to understand the collective behaviour patterns of users and ways to interpret them is a well-understood process for some professions. Marketing professionals in particular tend to have an innate understanding about the effects of social

---

[44] Omand, D, Bartlett, J, Miller, C. (2012). #INTELLIGENCE. Demos. Available from *www.demos.co.uk/files/_Intelligence_-_web.pdf?1335197327*

media and its influence on behaviour. Of the many excellent works within this field the book *33 Million People in the Room*[45] states three core principles concerning social media that are particularly relevant for the Internet investigator:

1. Different types of (social) networks exist for different audiences and different purposes, and each *is a microcosm unto itself:*
   a. *Relevance to the investigator*: most persons of interest will have accounts on more than one social media platform to reflect different aspects of their personal and professional lives, e.g. Facebook for friends and family, LinkedIn for professional advancement.

2. There is no one size fits all solution to social networking and each social network is created with *different users and uses* in mind:
   a. *Relevance to the investigator*: different strata of society use different social media platforms for different purposes, e.g. Bebo is targeted at the teen and young adult market, whereas LinkedIn is intended for the established professional market. The point of this is that the investigator can expect different persons of interest to have different social media accounts depending upon factors such as age, gender, social status and profession.

3. A *fundamental understanding* of the differences between networks is key to making the best use of the tools:
   a. *Relevance to the investigator*: think of each social

---

[45] Powell, J. (2009). *33 Million People in the Room: How to Create, Influence, and Run a Successful Business with Social Networking.* Financial Times Press; 1st edition (February 10, 2009)

media platform as a unique self-contained world within itself, with a distinct set of rules and customs that any new interloper is required to learn to be effective within that environment. This point has specific repercussions for aspects of an investigation such as security; some social media platforms such as LinkedIn allow account holders to see who has viewed their account whereas others such as Facebook do not. Knowing the suitable technical nuances between social media platforms distinguishes the seasoned OSINT professional from the more novice Internet investigator.

To highlight some of these points in more depth, shown below are several of the main social media platforms:

Platform name	Platform description	Intended audience	Data validation rules?	Number of users (2014)/yearly growth rate (where available)	Target language/ regional focus	Interest to the investigator
Facebook	Text- and image-focused platform but with some more advanced mapping and instant message functionality coming online	Possibly the most generic of all social media platforms in that it is intended to capture the social life of users from the very young to the very old	Some verificatio n of users via phone and external email, but aside from that very little	1,310,000,000 /22% 2012– 2013[46]	Predomina ntly European and North American but rapid penetration into developing regions such as India, Africa and Russia as user base grows	The first port of call for almost all investigations as this shows the personal life and connections of a person of interest

---

[46] *www.statisticbrain.com/facebook-statistics/*.

LinkedIn	Similar to Facebook but with a cleaner, more streamlined look (white space is king on this platform). Users have the ability to list résumés on the site and create and join specialist interest groups	Business-minded Professionals	Some verification with regard to types of qualification, e.g. medical degrees from certain schools and certain requirements to create business-specific pages and members groups	313,000,000[47]	European but with growing user groups in the Americas and the developing world	Very useful for investigations involving persons of interest who have to maintain an outwardly respectable persona (typically fraudsters). If profiles for the same individual can be found on both LinkedIn and Facebook then the investigator can often build a very comprehensive picture of that person of interest
Tencent QQ	More of an amalgamation of social media tools such as instant messaging, email-style chat and game playing that has grown out of this platform's original	Technologically minded Chinese youths	Previous requirements for a People's Republic of China identity card number; however, this is no longer needed to gain an account on	200,000,000[48]	Initially deployed in the People's Republic of China, but increasingly popular in the wider Pacific Rim region. An English	Very useful for geostrategic researchers looking to gain access to difficult to reach populations in the Pacific Rim area

[47] www.statista.com/statistics/274050/quarterly-numbers-of-linkedin-members/
[48] www.techinasia.com/qq/

	roots as an instant messaging tool		this platform		language version may see the platform gain wider use.	
Twitter	A microblogging site allowing messages or 'tweets' of 140 characters or fewer. Trends are created with the now eponymous 'hash tag' (#)	Technologically minded youth and those used to communicating in shortened 'text speak'-style prose. Breaking through to celebrity and mainstream users	None	271,000,000 active users per month[49] (highly volatile user group, hence uncertainties about true number of users)	Initially English but quickly spreading across many language spheres	This platform is of particular interest to geopolitical analysts due to its role in the so-called 'Twitter Revolutions' and the popularity of this platform with extremists of all persuasions
Deviant Art	A digital art gallery for aspiring artists to post their work and connect with other likeminded artists and fans	Digital art community	None needed; anonymity preferred	1,000,000[50]	Anglophone	Even though 99 percent of the work on this platform is legal, there have been instances of more suggestive works being placed onto the site with the intention of signalling to certain viewers the presence of

---

[49] https://about.twitter.com/company
[50] www.quantcast.com/deviantart.com

						more hardcore images on request
Myspace	Strong focus on music with a social network built around fan groups (co-owned by musician Justin Timberlake)	Teen and young adult market	None	36,000,000[51]	Anglophon e	Often used by paedophiles to groom and connect with victims
Tumblr	Somewhat like Twitter but longer-form blogs including images	Teen and young adult market with a strong bent to the creative market	None	300,000,000[52]	Multilingu al	Popular with protest groups and other semi-legal groups

The preceding list is by no means an exhaustive one of all the current social media platforms; indeed there are several hundred general platforms and thousands of smaller niche-interest platforms on the web. The reason for examining these platforms in particular is that they all reveal a specific aspect of social media technology in general.

The examples of Facebook and QQ underline the principle of cyber geography and how the user group, even for the largest social media platforms, is very specific to both the geographical and linguistic spheres. Platforms such as

---

[51] *http://expandedramblings.com/index.php/myspace-stats-then-now/#.U_J3CpRdU00*
[52] *http://allthingsd.com/20130521/how-many-users-does-tumblr-really-have/*

LinkedIn, when compared to Twitter, show how the different functionality of a platform can affect the types of data that can be available across different social media sites. DeviantArt shows how the scalability and anonymity of social media technology can be used to hide sinister content. MySpace shows how designers of different platforms aim their products at different demographics broken down by factors such as age range, gender and social status. When comparing all the platforms together the different formats of data that social media technology collectively produces (e.g. images for Tumblr, text streams for QQ and so on) becomes obvious.

Like looks for like, and like likes what like finds

This curious phrase encapsulates the way that the Internet facilitates the development of connections between individuals with extremely niche interests and viewpoints. Niche-interest groups can form on mainstream social media platforms as well as bespoke social media sites dedicated to an interest. One such niche-interest site was titled Cannibal Café and services users who fantasised about human cannibalism. It was on this site that Armin Meiwes successfully advertised for a victim to be willingly killed and eaten by Meiwes[53]. The Meiwes case, aka The Internet Cannibal, has now become possibly the most notorious example of the Internet's ability to connect individuals with interests even at the most extreme fringes of normal human behaviour.

By examining even just this one aspect of OSINT, the core themes outlined at the start of this book concerning cyberspace (multilayered, cyber geographies, mixed medium, tangibility) become obvious. The question is: how to make sense of this space and start to effectively investigate it?

The core principles of networks and how they affect investigations on Deep Web social media platforms

---

[53] http://news.bbc.co.uk/1/hi/world/europe/3230774.stm

One of the main drivers behind the incredible success of social media is that it exploits people's natural tendency to form networks based upon shared interests and values.

Within the context of social media technology, networks are created by the connection functionality inbuilt within all social media. The exact form that the connection functionality takes varies between social media platform, e.g. 'Friends' in Facebook, 'Circles' in Google Hangout. However, the symbolism of a connection between users is the same, i.e. that two connected users have a closer relationship than the other unconnected users on the same platform.

Networks form around almost any form of human interest, from the benign to the most extreme forms of criminal and terrorist activities. What social media technology allows is the creation of networks that are free from the traditional constraints on network size such as geography and the number of people another person can canvass for similar interests within a certain period of time. As such, when conducting an investigation within a social media web environment, a key shift in thinking for an investigator accustomed to investigations within the physical world is that within the Deep Web the best approach is to focus on investigating networks as opposed to just focusing purely on the web presence of individuals.

As an example of the necessity to shift away from targeting individuals to targeting networks within the scope of an Internet investigation, consider the following scenario. Imagine you are a geopolitical analyst tasked with assessing the organisational stability of a country's governmental system. One approach you could adopt would be to look for signs of discord and interpersonal tension within the Twitter feeds of the ruling party. The government you are looking at is typical of the Western model of government in that any public or media relations are closely controlled by a centralised media team; as such, the Twitter feeds of the ruling parties' elite (President, First Minister and so on) present a homogenised 'on message' flow of not very insightful content. However, the ministers on the periphery of the party will typically provide a far more representative view of how things really are within the party, as they are free from the tight controls on central party members or lack the staff resources to have someone else manage their social media feeds. This theoretical example of investigating the core of a network by examining the data generated by those individuals on the periphery of that network is a technique used by investigative professionals since well before the dawn of the Internet. However, given that the concept of network building is integral to social media technology, the idea is clearly worth restating.

**Look for the weak link: principle in action**

Shown in this panel is a self-portrait of Alexander Sotkin, a Russian soldier who posted multiple images of himself on the social media platform Instagram circa July 2014. The images, with accompanying messages, apparently showed Sotkin servicing Russian military mobile surface to air missile platforms, from various locations in Ukraine. The images posted by Sotkin ran completely contrary to official Russian Government claims that there was no large-scale deployment of Russian troops within Ukraine at the time Sotkin was posting the images.

Given the hostilities that were occurring within Ukraine at the time and that the Malaysian Airlines flight MH-17 had been shot down by a surface to air missile system, fired from disputed Ukraine territory on 17 July 2014, Sotkin's photo posts were politically incendiary when they were released.

This example is just one of many of how one individual's actions, facilitated by social media, can compromise the operational security of an entire organisation engaged in a clandestine activity

---

The two essential principles when seeking to investigate any network are target the weak link to gain access to the network and then laterally move through the network to gain access to the target information or individual:

1. _Target the weak link_: within any network of people (especially one engaged in nefarious activity) there will always be one individual who cannot help posting revealing information about themselves and the activities of the rest of the network, and in so doing compromises the operational security of that group. For the

investigation the challenge is not so much locating this individual,[54] but ascertaining how many degrees of separation the indiscreet individual is from the core person of interest. Once the closeness or distance between individuals within a network has been ascertained, the investigator is then in a position to draw inferences about the relevancy of the data gained from a third-party profile to the core person of interest within an investigation. Think of this stage as finding the initial thread of an investigation.

2. *Move laterally through the network*: the goal of this stage is to move through the target network to reach the final objective of the investigation. This could be as specific as connecting to the profile of a person of interest or as general as moving about a network to find all the connections to certain key persons of interest. Many social media platforms such as LinkedIn present barriers to unrestricted lateral movement, meaning that users can only form connections with other users if they are within a couple of degrees of separation. These technological barriers necessitate a 'softly softly' approach to movement within a network as the investigator connects to users' profiles that allow further penetration into the target network. In addition to the technological challenges, there are a couple of methodological issues that the investigator needs to be mindful of when moving through a network, namely which connection is a pathway deeper into the network

---

[54] I have successfully investigated networks involved in drug running, contract killing, sectarian violence, terrorism, espionage and prostitution rings, and in every case there has always been at least one member of that network who has been so indiscreet about themselves and their co-conspirators that I have been able to worm into the network and fully illuminate it. The 'weak link' is always a fixture of any network.

(good) and which connection will lead the investigator out of the network and into a dead end (bad). This process of assessing who is connected to who and for what reason requires a level of judgement from the investigator, as all people active on a social media platform are ultimately all connected to one another if the network is expanded wide enough[55].

Theory into practice

Just as the meta search engines discussed in *Chapter 2* allowed the investigator to throw a wider net over the Surface Web than merely going directly to single-source search engines as a first port of call, so there are a number of useful meta search engines that allow an investigator to query multiple social media platforms:

Tool name[56]	Freeware?	Social media platform(s) tool focuses on	Functional description
Social Searcher[57]	Yes	Facebook, Twitter and Google+	Provides a clear side-by-side display for search terms from Facebook, Twitter and Google+
TweetDeck[58]	Yes	Twitter only	Allows the investigator to view

---

[55] Frigyes Karinthy developed a theory that every person on the planet is connected by six or fewer degrees of separation. Although the theory has been challenged and refined over the years, the basic principle is that everyone can be connected if you expand their personal network enough. The risk this poses to any investigation is that false links can be created between people who are only distantly related.
[56] Due to the volatile nature of the technology that is used to build social media sites, many of the preceding social media meta search engines are often offline as the makers of the tools struggle to keep up with the rapidly changing technology used by social media companies. The solution for the investigator is not to rely on one tool but to develop skills in a number of tools.
[57] *www.social-searcher.com/*

			the content of multiple accounts simultaneously. Additionally, this tool now runs within the browser, therefore not requiring an install of specific software that may be barred within some public sector organisations
Social Mention[59]	Yes	Does not specify but would appear to pull from a broad range of social media tools	Very useful for keyword monitoring of trending topics. Also has the useful function of allowing an export of search results to CSV/Excel format
IFTTT[60] (If This Then That)	Yes	Facebook, LinkedIn and Email[61]	A very powerful tool that lets users specify actions based on conditions that occur in data: If [condition occurs] then [take this action]. Can be used for a number of useful purposes such as searching Facebook for the occurrence of certain images and so on
One Million Tweet Map[62]	Yes	Twitter only	World spot map view of Twitter posting. Has the ability to allow users to filter Tweets based on postcode and keywords

Aside from increased coverage of the Deep Web that the preceding meta engines provide, the tools capture a unique feature of the way people use social media technology in general. As *33 Million People in the Room* states, different social media platforms exist for different purposes and this by implication leads to the conclusion that a single person of interest will have accounts on multiple social media platforms, all fulfilling different social needs (Facebook for

---

[58] *https://tweetdeck.twitter.com/*
[59] *www.socialmention.com/*
[60] *https://ifttt.com/wtf*
[61] Many social media platforms will offer updates via email. As such, IFTTT can be used to filter these incoming emails.
[62] *http://onemilliontweetmap.com/*

family and friends, LinkedIn for professional contacts and so on). By using social media meta search engines the investigator is given a far more strategic view of an individual's web presence, and crucially, this allows the investigator to cross-reference different profiles on different social media platforms to build up a more coherent picture of a person of interest's digital profile.

"So social media is the Deep Web?"

Well, no, not entirely. Although social media technology creates a huge amount of Deep Web content, much of the Deep Web is made up of content generated from non-social media platforms. The important point is that Deep Web content is not searchable by mainstream search engines, irrespective of whether this content is generated by social media platforms or some other form of web publishing mechanism.

Platform-specific search tools

Separate from the tools that aggregate content from multiple social media platforms are the tools that can focus solely on just one. The advantage of these tools over the meta tools is that although both classes examine the same content, one-platform specialist tools often retrieve much more metadata that can be analysed in creative ways. Data derived via specialist tools can be used to generate insight such as the time zone that the user of an account is based within, the average distribution of posts over a given time period and even the psychological profile of a given user. Used appropriately and dependent upon the context of the investigation, these facts can provide great insight into the habits and behaviour of individual users that can prove useful to the OSINT researcher.

What can be gained from metadata analysis?

As part of a research project looking at social media use by extremist groups active in Sub-Saharan Africa, the Author gathered a large number of statistics derived from the metadata attached to more than 150 extremist websites. Two pieces of data that were collected for every Twitter account within the study's dataset was the number of followers of the site and the number of sites that account was following. Analysis of the data showed an interesting relationship to the follower/following ratio, which for the standard Twitter user is on average about 1 to 1, i.e. for every one person who follows an account, that account will either reciprocate the follow or find someone else to follow. The ratio for the extremist Twitter accounts was typically 0 to 1, i.e. they followed no one even when they themselves often had thousands of followers. This observation, coupled with the fact that the extremist Twitter accounts almost never retweeted someone else's posts, indicated that extremists use the Twitter service as a broadcast medium for propaganda rather than a place for conversation and debate that the service was intended to provide. The full report can be read at this link[63]. However, for the purposes of this book the key point to understand is that this kind of insight can only be gained by taking an analytical step back from the raw data and by comparing data across multiple accounts. By doing this, patterns and deeper nuanced analysis typically emerges.

└───┘

The following are specialist tools that can be applied to various social media platforms:

Tool name	Freeware?	Functional description	Social media platform(s) tool focuses on	Situations where this tool is useful for the investigator
NodeXL[64]	No charge for tool, but user must have a copy of Microsoft Excel (2007 or 2010) and Windows (XP, Vista or 7) for the add-on to	Focuses on mapping the social networks between users across various social media platforms	Can retrieve network data from Twitter, YouTube, Flickr, email (.pst files), Facebook, Exchange, Wikis and WWW hyperlinks (easily the most comprehensive	Useful for mapping special-interest groups that span across social media platforms, e.g. protest groups and so on

---

[63] Bertram, S and Ellison, K. (2014). Sub Saharan Africa Terrorist Groups' Use Of Internet. Journal of Terrorism Research Volume 5 Issue 1. Available from *http://ojs.st-andrews.ac.uk/index.php/jtr/article/view/825/704*
[64] *http://nodexl.codeplex.com/*

	work		tool featured within this chapter)	
Lococitato[65]	Users charged for software but very modest fee (<£100) for download	Focused purely on mapping Twitter relationships, including follower relationships and retweets	Twitter only (makers do produce an equivalent piece of software that maps Facebook networks; however, this is only available to law enforcement)	Mapping the flow of memes between Twitter users as well as the day-to-day work of looking at who is following who
Maltego Tungsten[66]	Users charged for software	A very powerful tool for the advanced user allows automated analysis of network infrastructure as well as many features around social media platforms. Comes complete with own easy to use scripting language	Twitter, YouTube and Facebook are all included along with a huge number of functions that can be applied to Surface Web sites	Particularly useful for an investigation involving a large crossover between Surface Web and Deep Web platforms
TweetPsych[67]	Free web-based tool	Draws up a psychological profile of a Twitter user based on their tweets[68]	Twitter only	Useful for a strategic view on the sentiment in a user's tweets e.g. positive, negative and so on
Snap Bird[69]	Free web-based tool	Retrieves all a user's tweets, even ones posted to a separate user profile	Twitter only	Very useful for providing a complete picture of a user over an extended period of time. A specific tool for

---

[65] www.lococitato.com/
[66] www.paterva.com/web6/
[67] http://tweetpsych.com/
[68] Many professional psychologists would challenge this tool's ability to construct an accurate profile on an individual based on such limited data. I leave the final decision over its validity to your judgement.
[69] http://snapbird.org/

				use on profiles that are identified as belonging to persons of interest
TweetStats[70]	Free web-based tool	Provides a statistical analysis of a user's Twitter activity based on time of day, date, posting frequency and so on	Twitter only	Useful when considering attribution of a Twitter account to a specific time zone or user demographic, e.g. if all posts are Monday to Friday 9 am to 5 pm US Pacific time, it is a fair assessment to make that the user is based in Pacific America and is posting from work

These tools give a small flavour of the types that can be applied to various social media platforms. Although there is a focus on Twitter in the preceding list, new tools that can be used on other platforms are published almost daily.

The important point to take away from these tools is that social media platform-specific tools – when used correctly – can give a far more granular picture of a specific social media account than the 'top-down' strategic view that more generic tools provide. Finding and effectively applying these tools is largely up to the investigator, as any published list is out of date almost as soon as it is published due to the rapid pace of social media technology in general.

---

[70] *www.tweetstats.com/*

The importance of identity online

One assumption that many novice investigators make is that everyone who is online wants to be anonymous – this could not be further from the truth. There are many thousand of examples of individuals being highly overt about associating online content with their identity; indeed tangible financial rewards can be created on social media platforms such as YouTube by creating a following around a well-defined web identity. Of course users are not required to stick to their given physical-world identity within cyberspace, but even when users fabricate online personas there is often a strong incentive to maintain this persona over years or even decades.

The reason behind this behaviour maps back to our most basic human desire to be accepted and respected within a social group, and this trait affects us just as much in the digital world as it does in the real world. The work of cognitive anthropologists Jean Lave and Etienne Wenger (Lave & Wenger 1991)[71] is particularly useful for understanding clustering around social media resources, specifically with regard to their concept of a 'Community of Practice' (CoP). In Lave and Wenger's original theory[72] CoPs were defined as groups of individuals who share a trade or some distinct profession. This common interest unifies the group and motivates the group to acquire more knowledge on the subject that the group is themed on. Although Lave and

---

[71] Lave, Jean; Wenger, Etienne (1991). *Situated Learning: Legitimate Peripheral Participation.* Cambridge: Cambridge University Press. ISBN 0-521-42374-0.; first published in 1990 as Institute for Research on Learning report 90-0013.
[72] The concepts surrounding Communities of Practice have evolved significantly since Lave and Etienne's original work. The original concept is used here for its applicability to open source research as opposed to providing an overview of the current thinking about CoPs.

Wenger originally developed the concept based on an observation of tradesmen active in the physical world, the theory is just as applicable in explaining group behaviour on the Internet.

✎ Leetspeak

Certain CoPs go so far as to develop their own versions of languages. The most well-known example of this is Leetspeak, which uses a combination of letters and numbers to create a version of the English language that can only be written. Originally the sole preserve of a hacker, Leetspeak has been adopted by others on the Internet, particularly to create very 'sticky' usernames. Try investigating the background of th3j35t3r (The Jester), a notorious cyber vigilante who has pursued a multiyear campaign against online Jihadists.

Within CoPs online there almost always develops a hierarchy of user, whether the topic of interest for the forum is benign or malicious in nature. Once a hierarchy has been established within a forum, those at the top tend to want to impose that respected and powerful status on other similar-interest groups spread across the Internet. The easiest mechanism for doing this, which avoids a lengthy climb from obscurity, is to reuse a distinctive username across multiple social media platforms.

By joining the dots between forums the investigator has the potential to create a comprehensive profile on an online identity. There are tools that facilitate this process and although they were created to check the availability of a username across multiple social media platforms, they work just as well for tracing the reoccurrence of a username across the Deep Web. Two recommended tools are:

1. *http://knowem.com/*

2. *http://namechk.com/*

Final theoretical points

Levels of connection and volume of data

You might have noticed that while attempting some of the techniques within this chapter, the quantity of data that a person of interest's profile reveals depends largely upon whether the investigator's profile is connected to that person or not. This observation reveals the basic principles that apply across almost all social media platforms: the more connected an investigator's account is to a profile, the more data will be revealed to the investigator. Clearly the obvious approach to social-media-based research is to connect to as many profiles as possible during an investigation; however, this approach is not without its risks.

Figure 10 shows the three levels of connection that two profiles can have on a social media platform (the table on the left) mapped to the operational risk, information gained from the level of connection and level of effort on the part of the investigator to maintain the profile used to connect to the person of interest (the triangles on the right):

Level	Profile on social media platform?	Logged in to social media platform?	Connected to person of interest's profile ?
1	No	-	-
2	Yes	Yes	No
3	Yes	Yes	Yes

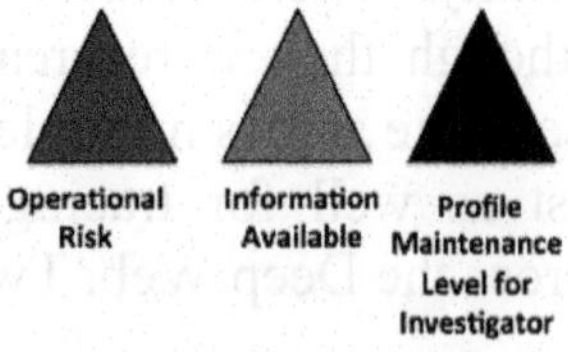

Operational Risk | Information Available | Profile Maintenance Level for Investigator

Figure 10: Three levels of connection available within a social media platform mapped to the risk level and the information

**that can potentially be gained (width of triangle represents
level of risk (left triangle), volume of data (middle triangle)
and level of effort to maintain the profile (right triangle))**

On first review of *Figure 10* you may wonder what the
operational risk triangle represents and why it is increasing
across the connectivity levels. The width of the triangle
literally represents the amount of risk that a connectivity
level presents to the investigator within the context of an
investigation. The risk level increases due to the fact that
when an investigator conducts activities on social media
platforms (creating and connecting profiles and so on), the
investigator in effect moves closer to the person of
interest's profile, going from distant observation at Level 1
to the digital equivalent of a direct conversation at Level 3.
Functionally this requires the investigator to create a fake
profile or 'sock puppet' that requires a credible backstory to
make the profile appear authentic (Annex A gives some tips
on best practice for building credible fake profiles). The
closer an investigator gets to a person of interest, the more
this backstory (or 'legend' to use classic intelligence
tradecraft speak) comes under greater scrutiny by the
person of interest. This level of contact requires great focus
and concentration on the part of the investigator and any
slip in the sock puppet's legend or behaviour can lead to
operational compromise (this concept is covered in more
depth in *Chapter 5*).

Taking the risk factor into account, examining *Figure 10* in
detail shows that at Level 1 (no profile, not logged in or
connected) the least amount of data is available from a
profile. Although revealing the least amount of data, an
investigation operating at Level 1 is the least risky of the
three levels as it does not require a profile to be created on a

social media platform that could alert the person of interest to the investigator's activities. This is the typical scenario when an investigator finds a social media profile of a person of interest via a Surface Web search engine and clicks on the link.

An investigator operating at Level 2 (profile and logged in but not connected) has a good mix of access to data versus the operational risk of exposure. As such, Level 2 tends to be the most common configuration for most investigations as this level hits the sweet spot that balances good access to data and a managed level of operational risk without undue levels of effort to maintain a relationship.

A Level 3 operation (profile, logged in and connected) gains the greatest amount of data, but incurs the greatest amount of effort from the investigator for profile maintenance as well as exposing the investigator to the highest level of operational risk. Typically this level of operation is carried out by specially trained personnel who have a specific remit to connect to identified profiles of persons of interest within the context of a much wider investigation.

Much can be gained from being a bold investigator in cyberspace, and I have participated in and am aware of many cases of high-level investigations involving the routine creation and use of a fake profile to connect to persons of interest. Linked with any online investigation involving social media is the possibility of compromise to the investigating agency. Although this possibility can never be 100 percent guarded against, a solid risk assessment by the investigator, taking into account the levels of connectivity outlined in *Figure 10*, is a measured and structured way to pursue an online investigation.

Conclusion

This chapter differed from the previous chapter in that the key to investigating the Deep Web is seeing beyond the raw information to visualise the social networks that created the web content in the first instance. Think of data within the Deep Web not as isolated islands, but as complex interconnected chains of information.

The skills required for effectively exploiting the Deep Web are heavily based in social science techniques such as social network analysis, content analysis and theories such as **Lave and Wenger's** concept of CoPs. The inquisitive investigator will find much material to develop their critical thinking with regard to Deep Web investigations in social science literature that examines group social phenomenon such as ganging, flash mobbing, closed communities and other forms of collective human behaviour.

✎ Message within the medium

Social media analysis is not simply about assessing the message communicated within a written text. Often large visual cues are present within the images that individuals and groups place onto the Internet. Take, for example, the image of Osama Bin Laden: what do you notice about the weapon he is holding and what does it mean to you?

The weapon in the picture is an AKS-74U, a 'stubby' variant of the more common AK-47 assault rifle. Bin Laden is carrying this weapon due to its status as a trophy item within the Jihadist community. The AKS-74U holds this status due to the fact that specialist Russian soldiers such as tank and helicopter gunship crews carried it. Possessing a weapon like this implies that the owner has been skilful enough in battle to acquire the enemy's weapons, adding to the power and status of the individual carrying it. This one example serves to show how contextual data can alter the message that an image is trying to convey[73].

---

[73] As much as the author would like to claim the credit for this clever analysis, I cannot. Instead, the reader should consult Chivers, C.J. (2010). *The Gun. The Story of the AK-47*. Page 383 for the original analysis that contributed to this piece.

CHAPTER 3: THE DARK WEB

The Dark Web is the most secretive and potentially dangerous of the three layers of cyberspace that this book examines. Only reachable with specialist pieces of browsing software, this is the layer of cyberspace that you were warned about. The Dark Web is the place where drugs and guns are for sale in eBay-style marketplaces, where thousands of images of child pornography are stored in Wikipedia-style sites and where the worst of terrorists and serious organised criminals gather in the virtual world. The most obvious category of OSINT practitioner who will venture into this space is the one who has a specific anti-crime or national security remit. However, the small group of professionals interested in the Dark Web is broadening. As the Dark Web grows, private sector counterintelligence professionals are increasingly exploring it for stolen intellectual property and compromised data within the myriad of underground marketplaces. Of the web spaces that have been examined so far, the Dark Web is much more about understanding the context of the content being presented and attributing this content to a physical-world identity, rather than the execution of the raw technical skills outlined in the Surface Web and Deep Web chapters.

What is the Dark Web and where did it come from?

Answering this question is more of a challenge than describing the technical features of the Surface Web or Deep Web. By implication, the term 'Dark Web' implies something sinister and hidden and a section of the web that cannot be accessed by a conventional web browser. However, a more exact definition beyond that remains elusive. One possible reason for this ambiguity is that the Dark Web has less been created in an explicit way, but has more evolved as searching and indexing technology has made other parts of the Internet more accessible to lower-skilled users.

It could be argued that before search engine providers such as Google and Yahoo arrived, the entire Internet was the Dark Web: users had to have explicit knowledge of the URL of the website they wished to visit. The arrival of search engines allowed users to search across the Internet based on thematic concepts, e.g. the search 'fish giblets' when entered into a search engine such as Google returns a list of websites based on the search term rather than what is within the website's URL.

Since the arrival of search engines many Internet users have sought to keep their web content hidden for a multitude of reasons. This change in user behaviour has evolved the Dark Web from a collection of sites that cannot be found by mainstream search engines to sites that are deliberately hidden from the indexing process used by search engines. This important difference informs an investigative approach to the Dark Web.

The importance of The Onion Router (TOR) to the Dark Web

If there is one piece of technology that has come to be a byword for the Dark Web, it is the TOR browser. In very basic terms the TOR browser is a web browser that has been configured to connect to a sub-network of relay computers called 'TOR Nodes,' which through the use of encryption masks the identity and web browsing activity of the user (shown in *Figure 11*).

Who made TOR in the first place?

Given the current notoriety of the TOR browser, it surprises many people to learn that TOR was originally developed by the United States Naval Research Laboratory in the mid-1990s, with the intention of providing secure Internet communication.. After its initial deployment to the public in 2004, TOR technology continues to be developed by groups such as the Electronic Frontiers Foundation and other freedom of speech groups. Given the irony of the original intentions behind the TOR project and its now undoubted role as a nexus for criminals and terrorists, TOR technology is just another example of how, as William Gibson put it, "...the street finds its own uses for things".

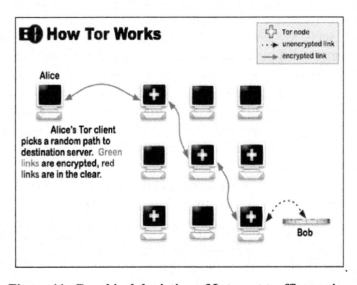

Figure 11: Graphical depiction of Internet traffic moving between layers of TOR nodes from the browser user (Alice) to the server (Bob) and back again

The exact details of the encryption algorithms used to

construct a TOR-based information architecture is beyond the scope of this book[74]. However, from an investigative perspective TOR allows an Internet user to do two things. Firstly, it allows them to hide their browsing activity from an Internet Service Provider (and hence any investigative agency with access to that ISP), and secondly, website publishers can configure their websites using the *.onion* suffix to only allow access to TOR users.

The .onion pseudo-Top Level Domain

Websites configured to only allow access to users using the TOR browser typically have the .onion suffix in front of the website address, in much the same way that Surface Web site such as .com or .net URLs are configured. The important difference between a .onion website and other Top Level Domain names (.com and so on) is that .onion sites are not true TLDs due to the fact that .onion sites are not included in the Internet's root directory[75]. From a technical perspective this means that any .onion site address can be cloned, but more importantly from an investigative perspective the lack of concurrency with the rest of the Surface Web places the .onion sites of the Dark Web even farther 'off the grid' than mainstream Internet usage.

Examining the relationship between that TOR browser and .onion sites in context shows that viewing the Dark Web as a place is not really accurate. In reality the Dark Web is a combination of web browsing and web surfing

---

[74] But are widely available to the curious with a quick Google search, even down to an exact transcription of the source code used within the current TOR algorithm.
[75] For those unfamiliar with this concept think of the Internet's root domain as the very top-level list from which all other Internet address are derived.

technologies, albeit technologies that have been designed to lean heavily towards the security of the users as opposed to ease of use or functionality.

So much for the theory – now what?

The first thing that any budding Dark Web investigator will need to do is to download a copy of the TOR web browser from *torproject.org/*. The 'Tor Bundle' is available for Windows, Mac and Linux-based operating systems and is an easy one-click install.

Is using TOR illegal?

This question has been asked many times, with the assumed answer being that even downloading the TOR browser is a criminal act. This is not at all true (in most parts of the free world), with the majority of TOR use being legal and the majority of TOR developers being open about their involvement in the project. A number of both public and private sector organisations discount the possibility of using TOR based upon the false assumption of its legal status. The author would encourage the reader that when considering the use of TOR within your organisation it is important to enter the use/don't use debate with all the facts and not just assumptions based on Internet shock stories.

Once the TOR browser is activated either by clicking on the desktop shortcut on Windows or activating the program via the Spotlight tool on a Mac, the Vidalia window is initially generated. This is a precursor step in the TOR process that connects the user's computer to a network of other TOR nodes[76]. Once this has successfully been done by the

---

[76] You might ask how your computer is now related to the TOR network. In effect, any computer that joins the TOR network becomes another TOR node and as such, TORified traffic is routed via the user's machine. All this content is encrypted; however, many

program a Firefox web browser is generated and the user is free to begin surfing the Internet.

It is at this point the user typically notices a number of things about the behaviour of the TOR browser. Firstly, although TOR uses the Firefox browser, there are no plugins allowed by the TOR bundle. The reason for this is that most plugins provide a gaping hole into your computer's security and almost always require you to give up your true IP address to provide their service. As such, this creates the basic rule that you should only use plugins if you do not care that your ISP knows who and where you are. Secondly, Google and other mainstream web browsers typically revolt when users attempt to access their services via a TOR browser. Google especially will prompt the user after almost every search to input a captcha[77] to prove that the user is not an automated piece of software called a robot. The objective of this approach on the part of Google and other mainstream search engines is debatable; however, the practical effect is to make using these search engines almost completely unusable with the TOR browser. The solution to this is to use products such as DuckDuckGo[78], a web browser designed to protect the anonymity of the user that plays nicely with the TOR technology. You will also notice that TOR is slow in returning results no matter what search engine the user loads into the system. This is due to the fact that the packets of data associated with the user's searching activity is being passed through three layers of encryption and via multiple TOR nodes. The fact that TOR works at all is surprising; the fact that it is

---

would-be TOR users feel deeply uncomfortable with the idea of their computer almost certainly facilitating the traffic of criminal content across the web.

[77] A captcha is a security process that gets the user to input and then validate a series of numbers and letters presented by the machine in an image file. The main purpose is to verify that the user is not an automated piece of software.

[78] *https://duckduckgo.com/*

slow is understandable.

Taking these factors into account, the initial impression of the TOR browser is often somewhat underwhelming and as one student on a course the author ran succinctly put it: *"The TOR browser and the Dark Web look like they were left over from the web of the 1990s."* This comment is not as throwaway as it may at first seem, as much of the technology that came after the year 2000 relied on identifying the user's IP address to create the rich multimedia content that we have come to expect from a modern web-surfing experience.

They don't know who I am! I can do what I want!

Not quite. Just because no one knows who you are does not mean that you are invisible. TOR browsing sessions still have an IP address (they must to receive data) and typically this IP address is listed as a 'TOR Node' on IP lookup services. In effect, using TOR is analogous to walking about with a mask on and although your identity is hidden by using a TOR service, you may tip off a target that you are looking at them. This concept is called making a target 'surveillance aware' and is discussed in more detail in the next chapter.

When faced with an apparent lack of functionality presented by the TOR browser, consider why you are using the browser in the first instance. If the objective is to hide the user's identity while browsing the Surface Web or Deep Web then there are better services to do this (discussed in virtual private networks in the next chapter). However, TOR's primary purpose is to provide the accessing mechanism for the Dark Web and allow access to sites using the .onion pseudo-TLD – no other browser does this.

Ticket to ride – now where?

With the TOR browser installed on their machine the

investigator has a vehicle to enter the Dark Web, but without access to the usual conventional searching technologies there is no mechanism to access unknown resources within the Dark Web space. The lack of search engines means that a user cannot browse the Dark Web in the way a user surfs the Surface Web. Instead, a Dark Web user must have the exact address of the resource they want to visit within the Dark Web.

It's worth considering the reasons why someone publishes content to the Dark Web as opposed to the Surface Web. The objective of a Dark Web publisher is the same as any other Surface Web publisher, in that both want their web publishing efforts to be read by others. The only difference between a Dark Web and a Surface Web publisher is that the Dark Web publisher is far more selective about the intended target audience. Most Dark Web publishers will want to strike a balance between security and informing their target audience of the existence of their resource.

Surprisingly, links to Dark Web sites are often published by their authors to the Surface Web. Try Googling phrases such as 'links to the Dark Web' and 'Dark Web links' and you will soon generate a sizable pool of links to .onion sites. In the past Surface Web sites advertising illegal services on the .onion domain have been low-key affairs; however, there has been a recent trend of formalising these Dark Web portals into much more accessible and permanent websites. The most obvious current example of this trend being deepdotweb.com, a Surface Web site that promotes, reviews and ranks many .onion sites selling illegal products.

 Be warned!!! – Click with caution!

Typically at the bottom of the Hidden Wiki page is a section called 'Hard Candy'. This is child pornography and even viewing these images in many (sadly not all) legal jurisdictions is illegal. The author cannot state enough how careful a user needs to be when exploring the Dark Web. Think before every click and remember that you are in a very different web space to the carefree Surface Web that you are used to.

Table provides a brief list of some of the most prominent Dark Web sites:

.onion URL	Name	Theme/services provided
http://kpvz7ki2v5agwt35.onion	The Hidden Wiki	Possibly the oldest list of Dark Web sites. Provides a list of other Dark Web sites based on theme
http://dppmfxaacucguzpc.onion/	TorDir	Another list site, possibly even older than the Hidden Wiki
http://thehub7dnl5nmcz5.onion	The Hub	One of the new generation list sites that adds a forum to the standard list of .onion websites. Very much the model for the future of TOR list sites with its slick presentation and intelligent use of technology

Figure 14: List of Dark Web sites

To view the contents of the preceding sites copy and paste the URL in an active TOR browser and hit Enter. This should resolve the site and allow the user to explore the resource like any other website. You may notice that many of the links in *Figure 14* and the Dark Web links found on the Surface Web are dead. This volatility in availability of Dark Web sites is due to the often-illegal nature of Dark Web site content and the paranoia of their publishers who tend to regularly move .onion sites to avoid scrutiny from law enforcement. Additionally Dark Web sites tend to be hosted on small computers that lack the redundancy and power of the commercial servers that provision the Surface Web and Deep Web. Both of these factors combine to create the 'here today, gone tomorrow' feel of the Dark Web.

 Top tip – even when using TOR, be very cautious about receiving files over chat or email services.

Various 'hacks' exist that exploit vulnerabilities in TOR. As an immediate suggested 'fix' for this issue, I recommend the online equivalent of what is termed in the language of classic intelligence tradecraft, a 'dead letter box drop'. This method involves two users having login details to a single email address (a disposable webmail address is best). One user logs on to the account, creates an email, attaches a file and then saves the email to the draft folder. The second user then logs on to the account and downloads the attachment saved within the draft email. This method avoids the direct peer-to-peer connection of computers that can reveal a user's true identity and should be used when the investigator does not trust a contact or is working undercover. As suspicion is the norm within the cyber underground, many players within this space would not take exception to these measures and in many cases, this process would add credibility to the investigator's adopted persona.

Possibly the key difference between the Surface Web and the Dark Web is that there is no centralised search technology like Google that allows the user to navigate the space using search terms. Instead, navigating the Dark Web is reliant on knowing the exact URL of the .onion site that the user wishes to visit.

Investigating the Dark Web

Conducting an investigation within the Dark Web is challenging. Unlike the Surface Web and Deep Web, if an investigator finds themselves within the Dark Web space within a professional context, chances are they are there for a specific reason as opposed to using the Internet to enhance an ongoing investigation, as is often the case with the other webs. Unfortunately, due to the opaque nature of the Dark Web the investigator simply does not have the tools available that an investigation in other parts of the web affords. Instead, the investigator must adapt two old investigative techniques to the challenges presented by the Dark Web.

1. *Follow the money* – many, if not most .onion publishers are engaged in Dark Web activities for one reason: money. Just as in the physical world, tracking assets can be an effective way to identify persons of interest within an investigation. On the Dark Web a form of currency called cryptocurrency reigns, and names such as Bitcoin and Litecoin have become synonymous with criminal activity.

   Part of the security aspect of cryptocurrencies is that all transactions are centrally recorded to preserve the integrity of the overall currency. The upside of this system is that it prevents one user inflating the relative value of one of their coins; the downside (for criminals) is that anyone can see any transaction that has ever occurred within the currency's network.

 How do cryptocurrncies work?

In simple terms cryptocurrencies take the core principle inherent to all currencies (scarcity and value to others) and adapt them to the digital age. A digital currency only exists in a virtual form and is stored in a 'wallet' on the owner's computer. Scarcity is created by the fact that only a limited number of 'coins' of a certain currency are available via a 'mining' process that involves solving an increasingly complicated mathematical equation. The essential break that cryptocurrencies make with the principles intrinsic to conventional currencies, is that cryptocurrencies are not backed by the physical resources (typically gold) that support the value of conventional currencies. Cryptocurrencies are typically being used by communities that have a decidedly 'counterculture' feel to them, and the wide-ranging distrust of the Western banking system has created a market for cryptocurrencies that would not have existed in more stable periods. The glue that holds a cryptocurrency together is a community of users who share a common belief that each of them will continue to value the cryptocurrency in the future.

Although this explanation shows how to map the passage of funds through a cryptocurrency like Bitcoin, it does not tell the investigator who is behind a cryptocurrency transaction or wallet. Attributing any aspect of a cryptocurrency to a physical-world person is a challenge and really the only practical way to do this is to follow the trail of the money within the Blockchain until a wallet hex surfaces on a blog or website. The co-occurrence of a cryptocurrency hex ID with contextual data allows the investigator to start working towards attributing the hex ID to a tangible identity using the techniques outlined in the previous chapters.

2. *Who knew what and how?* – the second technique that is effective in investigating activity within the Dark Web is to consider how knowledge of a website is being distributed. Remember that there is no searching function for the majority of the Dark Web and as such, visitors to a Dark Web .onion site must have previous knowledge of the URL of that site to visit it in the first instance. Investigating the mechanism via which knowledge of .onion URLs are disseminated typically moves an investigation closer to attributing Dark Web content to physical-world identities. The main example of this technique is the case of Ross William Ulbricht, the now imprisoned author of Silk Road, a notorious drug website that vended all manner of illegal narcotics to thousands of customers. Ulbricht was caught by the US Federal Bureau of Investigation due to his LinkedIn profile and other social media platforms on which he attributed himself to the site. The lessons from this are clear: seek to contextualise Dark Web data with Deep Web and Surface Web sources and apply the 'look for the weak link' principle judiciously. Finding out who

knew what and how about the Dark Web will almost certainly require the investigator to construct a false profile online. The ethics of doing this are discussed in the next chapter, and the practicalities of how to do this are outlined in Annex A: *Tips for building a credible sock puppet.*

Tor2web and the growth of the 'Borderlands'

It is technically possible to list a website with a .onion URL on the Surface Web in a way that it will be indexed and returned by a mainstream search engine. The technology required to do this is called Tor2web and involves a proxy HTTP server to provide a gateway to the TOR hidden services.

Tor2web works by allowing the user to substitute the .onion suffix with .tor2web.org, hence routing the HTTP request via Tor2web servers and allowing access to Dark Web sites. A point to note is that Tor2web does not affect the anonymity of .onion publishers; it does affect the visibility that third parties have on a user using Tor2web to access .onion sites.

Although Tor2web can be used to access any .onion site, relatively few publishers have used the service to publish .onion sites to the Surface Web, with most examples being either the relatively well-known .onion sites such as the Hidden Wiki or publicity stunts and pranks such as Assassination Market[79].

What Tor2web does demonstrate is that the boundary between the Surface Web and the Dark Web can be blurred,

---

[79] *https://assmkedzgorodn7o.tor2web.blutmagie.de/*. Currently offline as of writing this book.

which gives rise to the area of the Internet that the author calls the Borderlands. Whereas Tor2web blurs the lines through technical means, there is a class of website that challenges the Dark Web's reputation as the only vendor of illegal goods by being situated on the Surface Web and indexed by Google but still vending the classic Dark Web content (drugs, guns and so on).

Omerta.com is a prime example of this new brand of criminal website whose owners are taking advantage of bulletproof hosting services[80] and the sheer size of the Surface Web to hide in plain sight. Sites such as Omerta are unusual in that they have been indexed by mainstream search engines, but the designers of the site have provided no descriptive data (metadata) of the content of the site. The effect of this is that although users will be able to reach sites such as Omerta by entering the URL directly in a search engine, i.e. *http://omerta.com/*, they will not be able to find the site through conventional text searches, e.g. 'credit card fraud site,' 'purchase guns online' and so on. By configuring a website in this way, although word of mouth is required to spread knowledge of the site, the consumer base of the site is broadened due to the fact that potential customers do not require the TOR browser to gain access to it. This tactic of listing criminal websites on the Surface Web while keeping them obscured from casual web users fulfils the dual purpose of increasing the traffic for a criminal forum while obscuring the site from prying eyes. With the continuing exponential growth of both the Deep

---

[80] Bulletproof hosting is a hoster that provides space on the Surface Web and allows considerable leniency in the content that they allow their customers to host on their sites. Using either legal tactics or jurisdictional 'safe havens' to stay one step ahead of law enforcement, bulletproof hosting is a growing feature of the Internet and an indicator of how unruly it is becoming.

Web and Dark Web the intersection between these two areas of cyberspace, the Borderlands, will continue to grow in the future.

Conclusion

The Dark Web is how the Internet used to be in its infancy with no search technology, no stable hosting, no social media and no fancy graphics. As the rest of the web has moved on, the Dark Web has been left behind, in large part due to the fact that the users of this web space, for one reason or another, do not want the scrutiny that being indexed by mainstream search engines brings.

 No index for the .onion space – for how long?

Saying that there is no search technology for the Dark Web is not strictly true. The Grams[81] search engine that runs inside a TOR browser became active in early 2014 and allows users to search multiple .onion drug marketplaces in just the same way a Google browser allows access to any number of Surface Web sites. The .onion sites that Grams has access to is currently small, due to the fact the owners of each of Grams' .onion sites have to give explicit consent for the tool to access the site via a technical feature called an Application Programming Interface. As of writing this book the .onion sites indexed by the Grams service are a tiny handful of the wider .onion web space, hence why this search engine does not feature more prominently within this book. How long Grams and its client sites will remain a small-scale affair remains anyone's guess, but even the existence of such a service signals the growing confidence of cyber criminals that they can operate within the Dark Web with impunity, free from the scrutiny of law enforcement.

Investigating the Dark Web space is difficult, due to the fact that the techniques outlined in the Surface Web and Deep Web rely on the security vulnerabilities that a less security-conscious web has created. In place of the more

---

[81] *http://grams7enufi7jmdl.onion/*.

technical 'bells and whistles' techniques outlined in the previous chapter, when investigating the Dark Web the investigator uses the most basic of techniques: follow the money and who knew what and when. The objective of any Dark Web investigation is to find the point where a train of activity moves from the Dark Web and into the Surface Web or Deep Web; at this point more contextual data becomes available that can attribute a stream of web content to a physical-world identity.

CHAPTER 4: INTERNET SECURITY FOR THE SMART INVESTIGATOR

So far the author has sought to demonstrate the 'art of the possible' of a mature OSINT capability, and this book has paid little attention to the issue of operational security. This is partly due to the author's 'risk positive' approach to intelligence and investigative work in general, but largely due to the fact that to fully appreciate the risks associated with OSINT research one must fully understand the potential of the capability. You as the reader may at this point be asking: 'What are the risks involved in OSINT, and why should I care?'

The answer depends on how you are using OSINT and the risk that this use generates for you as an individual and your organisation. If you implement all the techniques discussed so far within this book then you are using the Internet in a way very few users in the world are. This style of usage is in itself unusual and marks the investigator out as doing something unusual on the Internet. This can in turn lead to a compromise of investigative activity due to the target of an investigation becoming aware that they are being investigated.

The most obvious effect of an investigator compromising online security is the degradation of the effectiveness of an OSINT investigation, as research subjects become aware that they are being examined (surveilled) by the investigator and start to take down digital evidence and worse in response (colleagues of the author have been physically intimidated as a direct result of their online investigations). Although this scenario is the most likely outcome of an operations security (OPSEC) compromise of an OSINT investigation, the most serious outcome of OPSEC failure is the fatal compromise of a trusted source. This statement may seem overdramatic, but a number of novice investigators within both the public and private sector have rapidly become immersed in serious investigations where the risk of serious injury to a source if compromised has been extreme.

Through employing a simple set of steps the smart OSINT practitioner can ensure the security of their operations and protect their sources. Developing a cast-iron approach to operational security requires a solid understanding of both the conceptual risks and technical solutions that are involved in security in cyberspace.

Security: two brief principles

Although security is a multilayered issue that is a sub-discipline of intelligence professional practice in its own right, it is appropriate to outline two essential principles that assist in contextualising the theory and techniques outlined in the remainder of this chapter:

1. *The triangle of security*: one of the most basic principles of any security system is that security comes with a price that is paid in functionality and ease of use. In other words, the more secure any system becomes, the harder it becomes to use and the less it can do.

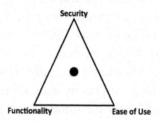

Figure 12: The balance between fuctionality, security and ease of use

The trick when imposing security on any system or workflow process is to strike a balance between the three corners of the triangle shown in *Figure 12*. Another important principle to note concerning the triangle model of security is that no system can ever logically be made 100 percent secure, as if it was it would have zero percent functionally and ease of use. As such, a compromise of security is inevitable and it is one of the skills of the OSINT practitioner to both expect this and plan for that day accordingly.

2. *Security as a multilayered defence*: security of any kind, be it physical, digital or procedural, is never one single bulwark against a threat. Instead, an effective security system comprises multiple layers of security that make up concentric rings around the asset that is being protected. The reasoning behind this approach is that it does not matter if one layer of security is breached, as a subsequent lower layer of security mitigates the threat. This principle is often described as the 'onion skin' approach to security.

Based on these two principles, the tools discussed in the next chapter are the building blocks for the layers of security, and the theory will assist in striking a balance between security, ease of use and functionality.

Creating a dedicated research infrastructure

For those who are committed to OSINT research and have identified it as a key component of an investigative programme, consider creating a dedicated group of computers and Internet connections that are only used for

OSINT work and are separated from the wider business network via a physical air-gap[82].

The reasoning behind this approach is based on an assumption and an assertion. The assumption is that sooner or later *all* computer systems will be compromised. The assertion is that by creating a 'standalone' research network the investigator creates a system that he does not *care* if it is compromised as all sensitive data is kept on a separate network (and hence not accessible to the network attacker due to the physical air-gap).

Giving away your identity on the Internet

Take a brief moment to review a visualisation of your Internet presence on *https://myshadow.org/visualisations*, a site that seeks to educate users on what data your computer gives out by default.

The basic issue surrounding anonymity (or lack thereof) of any system on the Internet is the identification and attributing by a third-party observer of activity associated with the investigator's system. The technical conduit for this process is via the IP address of the device connected to the Internet. As a very brief technical primer, an IP address is a digital postal address that allows systems to communicate with one another. Any electronic device can have an IP address and any device wishing to receive data must have an IP address to do so.

---

[82] A physical air-gap is a system via which there are absolutely no connections between two networks. This is the only 100 percent certain way that computer viruses and network intruders cannot move laterally across systems.

Exercise: Find your own IP address

If you have a computer connected to the Internet, it is a simple task to find your computer's own IP address. A Google of the phrase 'what is my IP address' will show the number that is your current IP address.

The issue investigators face around IP addresses is that the number is often clearly visible to a third party who has access to a web server log that clearly shows the time, date, duration of visit and IP address of anyone visiting that website (example shown in *Figure 13*).

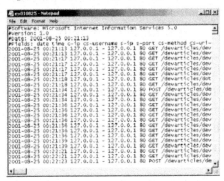

Figure 13: A typical server log showing the IP address of visitors to a web resource. A simple cross-reference with an IP lookup server will reveal visitor information such as geographic region and other data

This issue is compounded for public sector agencies by the fact that there are communities of people online who go to great effort to attribute IP address to well-known investigative bodies. This can lead to at best an embarrassing situation (*Figure 14*) and at worst a fatal compromise of an investigation.

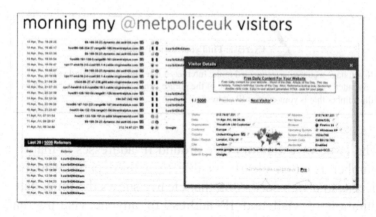

Figure 14: Server log posted on Twitter purportedly showing UK Metropolitan Police investigative activity on a third-party website

As it is not possible to surf the Internet without an IP address (that would be like trying to use the postal system without a postcode), this issue is not one of having your IP address discovered but rather that an IP address is not attributed directly to an investigator. The only sure way to do that is with a Virtual Private Network (VPN).

Going underground – Virtual Private Networks

Although VPNs were introduced with the TOR network in the previous chapter, a more technical examination of how VPNs work is worthwhile.

🛈 A cautionary tale

A student who attended one of the author's training courses shared an interesting story that planted the seeds of many of the ideas that this chapter is built upon. The student's background was as a human source handler for law enforcement, and his unit had been running a covert source within a serious organised crime group run by a very paranoid, very smart and very ruthless kingpin. Fearing (correctly as it turned out) that his criminal enterprise had been compromised by law enforcement, the kingpin created a large number of small one-page websites within long, complex, alphanumeric URLs that would not be found by accident and placed them onto the Dark Web. He gave each member of his organisation the address to one of these Dark Web sites with explicit instructions not to access them under any circumstances. The law enforcement unit's source within the criminal organisation dutifully reported the website address that had been given to him to his handler as just another part of his reporting of the criminal organisation's activities. The law enforcement agent in turn jumped onto the Dark Web and accessed the site using the TOR browser. Finding nothing of interest on the site, the agent logged off thinking nothing more of it. However, the kingpin reviewed the server logs related to each of the websites and saw that someone had visited the site; because each of the addresses he had given to his subordinates was unique, he was able to identify the leaks within his organisation. How did the story end? The source was never heard of again and that particular law enforcement unit learned that operational security with regard to OSINT wasn't trivial…

From the perspective of the user experience the Internet appears to be a collection of websites that are somehow interconnected by search engines. However, from a technological perspective the Internet is built from a collection of technologies that are mostly hidden to the user that allow the routing of data from the physical infrastructure that holds data (servers) to the physical devices that the user views data on (clients). The IP address is the first tangible glimpse that most users have of the hidden technical architecture that supports the Internet and it is this path from server to client that the savvy Internet investigator has to disguise.

In a conventional Internet connection scenario, data ('packets') are sent via clients and a server by ISPs. This system has worked well for the Internet for decades. However, this design was built for efficiency and not security. Thankfully there have been a number of projects to develop VPNs that prioritise the security of the user over raw functionality and although TOR is the first VPN service that has been introduced within this work, it is by no means the only option for the investigator.

At this point the reader might ask: *'Why do I need to use anything other than TOR, as it seems good enough for my needs?'*

To answer this question you should activate TOR and then visit a website such as infosniper.net or some other service that identifies a user's IP address[83]. Most likely this service will show a result labelling your IP address as a 'TOR Server' or 'VPN Proxy Server.' These results are what will appear when a paranoid web server administrator looks up the IP addresses that have visited the site that he is administrating. Although he won't know who has visited a site, he will know that an observer has been looking at the site who has been actively attempting to mask his identity. Even this small breach of OPSEC could be enough to make the subject of a research project surveillance aware, and compromise an OSINT investigation. Additionally any web server can easily be configured to bar access to browsers using TOR, potentially limiting the scope of an investigation.

 Running TOR via a VPN

It is possible to run TOR in conjunction with a VPN system. Doing this creates a multilayered security system and merely requires the user to activate TOR after the VPN connection has been established.

---

[83] A search of 'what is my IP address' via DuckDuckGo should return a large number of such services.

The key to solving this issue is (as ever) a measured risk assessment combined with a technological fix. The recommended software combination is:

- *Tunnelblick*[84]: a free piece of software that provides a useful graphical user interface for managing VPN connections. Tunnelblick is not a VPN itself, it's merely a digital 'socket' point for services like Perfect Privacy.

- *Perfect privacy*[85] *VPN services*: a paid-for service that allows access to a series of encrypted Internet relays that create anonymity and security via encryption. This service runs inside the Tunnelblick software.

The immediate advantages of using this software combination are obvious. Broadband browsing speed, unencumbered use of the Google search engine and free use of the Firefox browser complete with plugins are all noticeable improvements on the limitations of the TOR browser. Aside from the obvious, the more suitable benefits of the VPN/Tunnelblick combination is for the investigator seeking to access highly geographical regionalised sites on the Deep Web. Many cyber criminal gangs, especially Russophone ones, tend to bar access to any IP address that is not originating from a Russian-speaking geography. When using TOR, emerging from a Russian-based exit node is a matter of (slim) chance; however, the VPN/Tunnelblick combination guarantees an IP address of the user's choice and is the only real option for deep geographically based research.

---

[84] The exact installation and configuring of this software combination is up to you, as a verbose explanation of this process is unwieldy in print. If the installation help on the vendor websites is not sufficient, YouTube provides many installation tutorials for each piece of software.
[85] *www.perfect-privacy.com/*

The key point to take away from this section is that the utility of VPN technology lies in its ability to allow the investigator to blend in with the digital crowd, effectively hiding in the noise of the flow of everyday digital traffic. However, there is more to security and anonymity on the Internet than just blending into the crowd…

Advanced concepts of surveillance and detection

The applied surveillance theory and technologies this chapter has introduced so far has allowed the OSINT investigator to look like just another face within the digital crowd. However, there are scenarios where the investigator has to leave no trace of their online activities and where persons of interest can use asymmetric tactics to discover surveillance activity. To illustrate these points further a short thought experiment is useful.

 Private browsing – myth and fact

Private browsing, a function sometimes less charitably referred to as 'porn mode'[86], is a feature that prevents the browser remembering the history of the websites that the user visits. This feature has been present in almost all mainstream web browsers for the past few years, and the Chrome and Firefox browsers have the function installed by default. Many practitioners misinterpret private browsing as a panacea solution to the issue of security and OSINT research. To dispel the main myth, the software does not in any way hide your identity online. The core function of private browsers is to limit the records left on a computer of a user's online activity and different browsers achieve different levels of success at doing this[87]. Private browsing is of little use within OSINT professional practice, as leaving traces of digital evidence on a computer related to a legitimate research project is not an issue for the honest investigator. It is only featured within this book to convince you of the need for other technology.

---

[86] Trapani, Gina (May 4, 2005). "Safari's private (porn) browsing mode". Lifehacker. Retrieved 2010-04-11.
[87] *http://homepages.cs.ncl.ac.uk/feng.hao/files/DPM13.pdf*

Imagine a guard standing in a watchtower on a barren plain with a full 360-degree view to the edge of the horizon. There are two possible ways that the guard could become aware of an intruder:

1. *Scenario 1*: the guard observes an intruder walking up to the watchtower.
2. *Scenario 2*: the guard observes footprints around the watchtower, but sees no other signs of an intruder.

In both scenarios the actions of the guard after detecting an intrusion are irrelevant. The main point to take away is there are two ways an observer can become aware of an intrusion: direct observation of the intruder (scenario 1) and observation of traces of an intrusion without direct observation of the actual intruder (scenario 2). Common to both scenarios is that the guard raises the alarm, and the net result for the intruder in both scenarios is the same: mitigating action by the guard.

Although this experiment is abstract, there are clear parallels that can easily be drawn with OSINT professional practice. These are the obvious traces an investigative IP address left on a server log (scenario 1) and the less obvious indicators such as aggregated LinkedIn views (scenario 2). The issues within this section are somewhat challenging to conceptualise, but the technical solution is straightforward and more a case of using the correct technical approach at the appropriate time.

Avoiding direct observation (mitigating scenario 1): The only real solution to the issue of direct observation is not to be seen, and although being completely invisible in cyberspace is impossible (due to the IP address issue), a number of steps can be taken to prevent the investigator's

IP address appearing on a website's server log. These include:

- *Cache viewing*: although not obvious, Google employs a system called *caching* to store copies of the front page of a website within Google's own servers. The technical reasoning behind this is that caching speeds up web browsing; however, this feature allows the investigator to view a website without leaving a mark on the site's server log. Using this feature in Google is straightforward and merely requires the investigator to click on the small green triangle and then the 'Cached' text underneath the blue title of the search results.

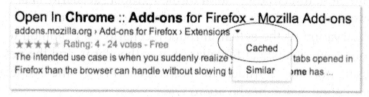

Figure 15: Cache viewing in Google

Note that when the page is displayed the URL is for a Google server and not the address of the site's home page. The investigator should be aware that if any of the links are clicked on the Google cached page, they will redirect to the site's proper server location that will start to leave traces of the investigator's visit as per normal web browsing. Passive Cache[88] is a useful Firefox add-on that combines Google cache and WBM results into one centralised display. Although not adding any more functionality, Passive Cache does increase the agility of the investigator when looking through multiple search results.

---

[88] *//addons.mozilla.org/en-us/firefox/addon/passive-cache/.*

- *Wayback machine (WBM)*: although Google cache viewing is useful for rapidly viewing singular web pages, it has obvious limitations for investigating whole websites. Fortunately for the investigator WBM's archive of websites often has a mirror image of a live website. These images can be explored without risk as the entire archived sites sit on the WBM servers.

To be categorical, both these techniques do leave traces of the investigator's IP address on servers (Google and WBM's systems); however, the chances of a person of interest being able to access the data of a secure third party like Google is highly unlikely[89].

By using techniques such as cache viewing the investigator is hiding behind someone else's digital wall to observe a website; however, the investigator should be mindful that being invisible is not the same as leaving no trace. There is a strong chance that an investigator can mask his identity using techniques such as VPN browsing, but still leave obvious digital traces of an investigation behind.

Leaving no trace (mitigating scenario 2):

Although a full enumeration of all the ways an investigator can leave a trace in cyberspace is beyond the scope of this book, it is worth looking at two specific examples of how online activity can leave obvious traces if one knows what to look for:

1. *Browser profiling* – take a moment to compare your web browser with one of your work colleague's. Notice

---

[89] Both Google and eBay have suffered large-scale data breaches in the past. However, these have most likely been the work of malicious hackers rather than the efforts of a person of interest attempting to uncover investigative activity directed against them.

anything different? Although it may not be obvious, nearly all web browser configurations are almost completely unique to a specific user, with the chances of an individual web browser configuration occurring on average only once per 286,777 samples[90]. This occurs due to the huge variations in the way users configure their web browser with features such as font sizes, plugins (remember *Chapter 2?*) and even screen resolution. All of these features are visible to a web server and a visit to *https://panopticlick.eff.org/* will return the almost unique fingerprint of the browser that you are using. What should be obvious is that an IP address is just one component of identity on the Internet and that relying solely on a non-attributable IP address to hide your identity online is analogous to putting on a pair of sunglasses before mugging a colleague and expecting not to be recognised. Defending against browser profiling is a challenge and there is no quick fix. The designers of the TOR browser have put significant effort into mitigating browser profiling and when the Panopticlick profiler page is visited using the TOR browser, the result is a reassuringly blank profile. Additionally the NoScript add-on[91] for the Firefox browser is recommended by the Electronic Frontiers Foundation as a way to limit browser profiling; however, it is by no means a complete solution. Of all the issues and fixes that this book addresses the subject of browser profiling remains the most open and unfinished, and is

---

[90] A study by the Electronic Frontiers Foundation found that of a sample set of 470,161 browsers 83.6 percent were instantly unique, with a staggering 94.2 percent of browsers with a Java Virtual Machine or Adobe Flash being identifiably unique with some processing. This fascinating paper can be read in full at *https://panopticlick.eff.org/browser-uniqueness.pdf*.
[91] *https://addons.mozilla.org/en-US/firefox/addon/noscript/*

an issue that the investigator must keep abreast of going forward.

 Going Dark: Turning off 'looked at' notifications

It is possible to turn of the 'People who have looked at your profile' notifications within the Linkedin service by going to the Privacy Setting of your profile. The downside of this is that the user of the profile cannot then view who has viewed their own profile. This technique is typical of many aspects of intelligence tradecraft in that an increase in operational security leads directly to a decrease in counter intelligence.

---

2. *LinkedIn clustering* – although the issue of the 'People who have looked at your profile' notifications in LinkedIn was touched on in *Chapter 3* along with the TOR browser and fake profile fix, there is another more suitable security issue within LinkedIn profile browsing. Have you ever noticed the 'People Also Viewed' column just off the right-hand side of the main display? The purpose of this column is to increase the 'stickiness' of LinkedIn with its user base, as theoretically the column allows users to view and link to professionals in similar industry sectors, hence making the overall service more useful for the user. The unintended consequence for the investigator is that the People Also Viewed column can tip off a group of persons of interest that they are being investigated. This situation occurs when a person of interest inspects the People Also Viewed column that relates to their own profile and sees other individuals who are involved in some kind of clandestine enterprise displayed in the column. A result like this is particularly suspicious for a person of interest if a group of profiles have been clustered together that do not have any obvious connection between them, such as direct links,

similar industries and skills, or shared groups. As is so often the case with individuals engaged in nefarious activity with a strong online presence (typically fraudsters), co-conspirators tend to be drawn from very different walks of life who would not naturally overlap in cyberspace. These individuals often go to great lengths to break and prevent connections between conspirators and as such, any links that do develop are often a dead giveaway that someone is on their trail. How LinkedIn goes about selecting which users' profiles should be displayed within the People Also Viewed column is propriety information; however, I would hazard a guess that profiles are clustered together based largely on the historical profile browsing behaviour of past users. Based on this assessment and my own research, even if the investigator is using a VPN service (TOR included) and a fake profile the clustering will still occur as the investigator's browsing activity is still originating from a single unique IP address. The only viable method to mitigate this threat is to change IP address for every profile viewed on LinkedIn. Although IP hopping is easily done within programs such as Tunnelblick and TOR, using this while attempting to browse multiple profiles can be a challenge. Remember the security triangle introduced at the start of this chapter? The 'ease of use' element of the triangle suffers dramatically when using this method.

/ **Just because you are paranoid...**

Over the years some have commented that the security steps in this book are excessive and overly paranoid. Validating the authors approach are a couple of case studies that show the risks to an investigator of compromise on the Internet, and a section of an entire industry that exploits lapses in the operational security of cyber investigators. In 2010 the Citizen Lab based within Munk School of Global Affairs in Toronto published a paper titled *Shadows in the Cloud*,[92] which examined cyber espionage activity emanating from the People's Republic of China against the Office of His Holiness the Dalai Lama in Tibet. *Shadows in the Cloud* showed that there had been a large-scale, multiyear cyber espionage campaign aimed not just at His Holiness the Dalai Lama but at a huge number of Western public and private sector institutions with the objective of stealing valuable intellectual property rights. The Toronto paper gave rise to a whole industry that attempts to prevent cyber espionage attacks, which has grown into a multi million-dollar subsection of the cyber security industry. One of the main techniques that this industry sector employs to discover new cyber espionage attacks is to examine the server logs of targeted companies for telltale IP addresses that trace back to China and give away browser configurations that use certain dialects of Mandarin.

Counterintelligence within OSINT

So far this book has concentrated on empowering the investigator to remain as unobserved as possible while conducting OSINT research. Although this does provide peace of mind during an investigation, for the most serious OSINT operations it is often useful to know who is attempting to observe your investigative activities online. This process of watching the watcher is called counterintelligence (CI) within the professional intelligence and security field. Although CI is well developed within the wider field of investigative professional practice, it is in its relative infancy within the world of OSINT. Despite this there are a few steps that the investigator can take to start building their CI capability.

The techniques outlined in the previous section attempted to create operational security by placing the investigator's

---

[92] *www.nartv.org/mirror/shadows-in-the-cloud.pdf*

IP address within a data repository that cannot be accessed by a third-party person of interest. Conversely the objective of CI in cyberspace is to provoke an observer into leaving their IP address within a database that the investigator can gain access to. The easiest way to do this is to create a website and embed a piece of tracking software into the code of the site and see who turns up. This process may sound complicated; however, there are multiple web tracking services such as StatCounter[93], which have been developed for sales and marketing purposes that allow site owners to track a site's user data such as number of visits and IP address of visitors. By creating a tracker the investigator is 'bugging' a website in the same way that a closed circuit television system observes a physical asset in the hope of catching an intruder. This technique is several degrees more technical than the other topics examined within this book, but it is not beyond the skills of the average IT support department or a few days committed Googling[94] on the part of the investigator. The really clever bit comes with what the investigator does next with the bugged website:

• *Tell everyone about it*: as many investigators have a prominent online profile, often with both a Surface Web and Deep Web social media presence, it is fair to assume that any observer will examine all obvious digital evidence relevant to the investigator. The obvious thing to do is to optimise the metadata of the bugged website to be picked up by a Google spider[95]. This in turn will

[93] http://statcounter.com/
[94] 'Hosting a website,' 'building a basic website' and 'embedding a stat counter' are all appropriate Google searches that will yield hundreds of websites to allow even the most non-technical user to complete this project.
[95] Once again Googling 'website optimisation' is a good starting point for

hopefully[96] allow the site to be returned as a top ten result when the name of the investigator is searched by the observer. Although this approach will reveal the IPs of users visiting the site, the inference or 'so what?' factor of the data this method generates will remain limited due to the highly public nature of the website. A more suitable and potentially more productive approach is to prevent the bugged website from being listed on any search engine index[97] but post the website link onto the social media profiles used by the investigator. Chances are the observer will be in 'click-happy mode' when examining the investigator's online social media profile and not think twice about clicking the link posted on the profile page. The instant the observer does this they will have revealed their IP address. The benefit of this approach over the initial approach of simply listing the bugged page on the Surface Web and then seeing who comes along, is that when an investigator gets a 'hit' of an IP address from a bugged website whose URL is only posted on a social media profile, the investigator can infer that an observer has specifically set out to examine the investigator's social media profile. The art of CI is to build a picture of the observer from the logical inferences that can be made on individual pieces of data. Getting creative with this technique can yield more useful counterintelligence:

o *Scenario*: a bugged website whose URL is buried several pages down on a Facebook page gets a hit from a TOR IP address.

---

operationalising this process.

[96] The more uncommon the name, the more chance it has of being picked up.

[97] Drop HTTPS from the URL and insert 'No Robot' text into the code.

- *Inference*: an observer who has made efforts to hide their identity has methodologically examined the investigator's Facebook page. It is unlikely that this would be a casual web user and this should tip the investigator off to start looking for other indicators of hostile surveillance.
  - *Scenario*: the investigator collates 'People who have looked at your profile' LinkedIn notifications with bugged website hits from a URL only posted on the investigator's LinkedIn profile. From this the investigator assesses that two LinkedIn profiles are being run from a single IP address.
    - *Inference*: an unknown observer is using social media sock puppets in an attempt to remain unobserved during surveillance activities directed against the investigator.

- *Tell no one about it*: the other option for conducting CI using a bugged website is not to list the site on Google or post the URL on any social media platform, but to clearly link the WHOIS details of the site to the investigator (the investigator's real name as the bugged site's registrant name and a prominent email repeated on the investigator's LinkedIn profile should be enough to do the trick). Any hit on a bugged site like this will be a slam-dunk indicator that an observer has taken the time and effort to cross-reference an investigator's details with the WHOIS database in an effort to find any new pieces of data on the investigator. In this scenario the inference that the investigator can draw from a positive hit on a bugged website is that an observer has good basic OSINT skills and is pursuing a rigorous course of research against the investigator.

Never log in to a personal email account on a research computer

Breaking this rule on the teams that I have managed and been employed within has been a cardinal offence. Why? Services such as LinkedIn rely on a business model that depends upon suggesting connections to users based upon their social network. Consider how these services become aware of these networks. As with all magical processes the trick lies within a sleight of hand that in this case is hidden within the small print of the user agreement of many social network platforms. Although the syntax differs from platform to platform, the sentiment is usually the same: if the user does not log out of the social media platform, that platform retains the right to monitor the activity of the user's computer. Data collected can include websites visited, preferences in stored cookies and even in some cases the content and recipients of emails being sent by the user. With this hidden treasure trove of data it is somewhat less surprising that some social media platforms can predict with such uncanny accuracy the connections that you make in your day-to-day life. The best way to mitigate this risk is to log out of social media platforms as soon as you have finished using them and never mix your own personal data within investigative data on a research machine.

Counterintelligence can be a frustrating pursuit, as the results are often enough to tell you that someone is observing you but usually not good enough to tell you who is observing you. Within the world of OSINT the CI techniques previously outlined may be just enough to warn an investigator who may be operating in a high-risk environment or managing a deep-cover covert human intelligence source that something is not right.

Encryption

It's worth reiterating that the closer an investigator gets to a person of interest within cyberspace, the greater the risk of compromise. Emails, online chat, profile links and developing following/follower relationships with surveillance subjects are all legitimate OSINT practices; however, all of these interactions dramatically increase the risk of compromise to operational security. As with many OPSEC issues there is no silver bullet for this issue, merely a combination of selected technologies and procedural checks and balances. The one essential technology integral to online security is the process of encryption.

At its very core the purpose of encryption is to stop unwanted observers viewing the content of a communication medium, be that an Internet connection (TOR), electronic document (email messages or attached documents) or online chat. The process of encryption utilises various complex mathematical algorithms[98] in a method that cyphers the data using a digital key to the degree that the original message can only be deciphered by using the original digital key. Encryption can be built into almost any device to serve a variety of security functions; the trick for the investigator is to use encryption in a way that increases the security of their interaction with a subject. Due to the complexities inherent in encryption, rather than using the convention used throughout the rest of this book of outlining tools first and then explaining ways in which the investigator can use them, for the next section I will outline a scenario and then introduce a tool that will mitigate the risk within the scenario.

The investigator should avoid

- *Having an email read by a third party*: of all the uses of encryption, encrypted email is probably the most commonly used but surprisingly the most difficult to configure in terms of software. The basic components required for encrypted email are outlined next; however,

---

[98] For an informed view on the mathematics behind encryption technology I recommend Bruce Schneier, an individual who has forgotten more about encryption and security than most people have ever known. Review his sizable web page on the subject (schneier.com/cryptography.html).

you will most likely have to consult the external 'how to' guides listed within the footnotes of the next section:

o Create a web email account with a third-party email provider[99] such as Hotmail or Gmail.

o If the reader is using a Windows-based system then download an email application such as Thunderbird[100]. If the reader is using a Mac, the default Mail program is adequate. Once synced[101] with the webmail account set up in the first step, the user will be able to download all emails from the webmail account onto the investigator's computer. This step is vital as the encryption and decryption functions are all carried out on the local machine and not within systems of the webmail provider.

o Download a version of Pretty Good Privacy, a free encryption program that has been developed specifically for desktop encryption. For Mac operating systems I recommend GPGTools (*https://gpgtools.org/*), and for Windows the Enigmail plugin for Thunderbird (*https://add-ons.mozilla.org/en-US/thunderbird/add-on/ enigmail/*. Users will first be required to download and install the Thunderbird email client).

o Configure encryption tools to work with the email program. The only semi-technical section of the

---

[99] There are security risks associated with using a webmail service such as Hotmail, and a bespoke server run by the investigator would be the more secure option. The reasoning behind using a third-party email is that if the concepts within this section are new to you then you will likely lack the technical ability to configure and run your own email server. The solution suggested within this section should be viewed as an introduction, not the final word on the issue.

[100] *www.mozilla.org/en-GB/thunderbird/*

[101] This is a very straightforward process within Thunderbird that merely requires the user to input the email address and password for the webmail account. If more instruction is required, YouTube has several hundred videos on how to set up a Thunderbird mail system.

installation process involves integrating the encryption tools into the email program. For Windows users this requires activating the Enigmail plugin within Thunderbird, which is done by accessing the 'Add-ons' menu within Thunderbird.

o Generate an encryption key. The final part of the process is to generate an encryption key specific to the machine that you are using the encryption software on. This is a straightforward process within both Thunderbird and GPGTools on Mail and merely requires the user to follow the key generation wizards integrated into each piece of software.

o An important point to stress concerning these encryption configurations is that all the cyphering is carried out on the local computer of the investigator. As such, if the investigator logs on to the webmail account from another machine, any messages sent would not be encrypted.

- *Having a document read by a third party*[102]: one very novel feature of most encryption technologies is to include an image file as a 'key' to the original source file. The encryption software takes the original source file and combines it with the key file to create a unique 'hybrid' file. As the encrypted file can only be decrypted by using the image key file, this tactic shifts the onus on the part of the intercepting agency from simply collecting target documents to collecting the cyphering key file as well. This tactic adds a significant layer of security to document transfers via the Internet.

---

[102] Although an email is technically a document, the process for encrypting a Word or PowerPoint slideshow is slightly different than the process of email encryption. As such, it is treated as a separate subject within this section.

- *Having an online conversation with a source read by a third party*: encryption technology is versatile and is not limited to just static forms of communication. Various algorithms can be used to cypher text chat and even voice conversations in real time. The advantage of this is clear: no third party can see what the investigator and the subject are discussing. Implementing encryption within text chat is relatively easy thanks to the Off-the-Record (OTR)[103] module that plugs into the Adium[104] (Mac) and Pidgin[105] (Windows) chat programs (Adium OTR comes inbuilt, whereas Pidgin needs downloading and then activating as a plugin). As with email encryption the message runs through the servers of a third-party server provider such as Google or Microsoft; however, the message text is encrypted and the decryption keys only sit on the conversation participants' computers.

- *Being seen having a conversation with a source*: classic examples of this scenario would be a journalist speaking to a source within an oppressive regime or a law enforcement officer making contact with a covert source within a serious organised crime group. In both these cases there are obvious and serious consequences of an unwanted third party observing the conversation. Although OTR would keep the content of a conversation secure, there would still be obvious evidence of the connection between the investigator and the source when using the Adium/Pidgin combination and even more forensic evidence of the contact if specialist tools were used. The solution to this is to take the conversation into

---

[103] *https://otr.cypherpunks.ca/*
[104] *www.adium.im/*
[105] *https://pidgin.im/*

the Deep Web with a program called Cryptocat[106]. The Cryptocat program is unique in that it only runs inside the Google Chrome browser, creating a chat room for multiple users. The beauty of Cryptocat is that it does not require the users to create profiles; they merely need to know the name of the chat room created by the first user into the room. As any user who knows the name of the chat room can enter that room, I advise you to apply the same principles for strong password creation[107] when creating chat room names. Of course there is a vulnerability within the Cryptocat system in that it requires all users to know the name of the chat room to enter it and passing the name of the room out via non-secure means can defeat the object of the exercise. The solution to this is to pre-plan a conversation or use alternate secure means such as crypto telephones[108] to disseminate the name of the chat room to all invited participants.

These encryption configurations are by no means the only ways that encryption can be used for security. Indeed the subject of what program is best for encryption and which programs have security vulnerabilities within them is a huge source of debate within the community interested in encryption issues. The preceding scenarios and solutions merely introduce the concepts of encryption.

---

[106] *https://crypto.cat/#*
[107] 20-plus characters, use of numbers, punctuation, capitalisation and special characters, i.e. <MyLittle,Chat.Room1873!!!?
[108] Hardware-based crypto telephones are still prohibitively expensive for the average user. However, an increasing number of smartphone applications allow encrypted voice conversation; examples include Cellcrypt (*www.cellcrypt.com/*).

Be warned: defeating encryption

The only practical way to defeat encryption is to intercept the communication before it is ciphered. This is actually very easy to do with today's modern crop of malware. Malicious worms and viruses such as Zeus and Poison Ivy have been around for decades and are either freely available or can be purchased for reasonable sums on the cyber criminal underground. As there are also large numbers of skilled hackers that will rent their services to any client, no questions asked, the risk to the investigator involved in a high-profile operation from a computer hacking attack is sizable and growing. The solution to this is to apply good computer hygiene standards and other security techniques such as black-boxing and dedicated research networks.

When using any form of encryption technology I advise practising with the tools before using them within a live operational situation. Remember that although encryption will increase the security of your documents, the ease of use and functionality of any encrypted documents will decrease. The basic principle that applies to any technology used within intelligence and security is don't roll out the door and expect it all to work first time, and it is within the high-pressure situations created by real-world cases that investigators are most likely to make small errors that can lead to an entire OPSEC breach. Practice, rehearsal and regular peer-to-peer training sessions on complex subjects such as encryption are a sure way to test technology and personnel and mitigate the risk of a breach due to lack of familiarity with the tools by the investigator.

Smart security – using the appropriate solution at the appropriate time

One point you may be confused about is what security technique should be used at what point in an OSINT investigation. Applying all the principles at all times, for all research projects, is an unworkable solution, as this system would favour the security aspect of the security triangle to the fatal detriment of the ease of use and functionality aspect of the equation. Instead, the investigator must select and apply the appropriate technology at the correct phase of an investigation. Doing this is somewhat of an art form that will develop in time, but the following matrix is a starting point for the investigator to base their security posture on.

Table 4: Threat level mapped to investigative activity

Type of activity being conducted by the investigator at this level	Threat level	Possible compromise scenarios	Risks associated with a compromise in OPSEC	Tools used at this level of risk
Casual Surface Web and Deep Web research	Low	Person of interest detects investigative activity on social media platforms	Organisational embarrassment and risk of reputational damage	Virtual Private Networks
Focused Deep Web research, casual interaction with persons of interest	Medium	Person of interest detects investigative activity in server logs	Possibility of more extreme response from person of interest, including legal action and acts of physical violence/protest	All of the above but consider using TOR browsing and conducting activity on a bespoke research network
Focused Deep Web and Dark Web research, deep interaction with covert human intelligence sources	High	OPSEC slip-up on the part of the investigator when communicating with covert source	Serious implications for all parties involved including threats up to and including risk to life	All of the above as well as encryption of email and online chat conversations. Consider counterintelligence operations to ensure OPSEC of this level of covert Internet investigation

CONCLUSION

"What can OSINT do for me?"

...was the opening line to this book. I hope you are now at least aware of how OSINT can benefit your professional practice, whatever that may be.

Documenting knowledge in writing is relatively easy, as is reading and understanding documented knowledge; however, turning abstract knowledge into tangible gains in professional practice is a challenge. This is the challenge that you now face: taking abstract concepts and lists of tools and rehearsing and reconceptualising them within a personal framework, so that they become integrated into the day-to-day professional practice of the investigator. It is within this process that many investigators become disenchanted with what OSINT can do for them, so I offer this final piece of advice for applying OSINT theory within a professional framework:

- *All OSINT techniques are not applicable all of the time.* Although this book has covered many search tools and several theoretical concepts that are applicable to OSINT professional practice, not all of these tools can be applied to every situation. Instead, a blended approach is needed that requires applying the correct tool at the appropriate time. The obvious question is how does an investigator know this? By identifying the web layer(s) (Surface, Deep and Dark) that is the focus of their investigation. From this point, identifying the correct tools and approach should be straightforward.

- *Do not attempt to memorise all OSINT techniques outlined within this book.* Try not to memorise the detail of a technique but concentrate on understanding the broader concept that underpins the technique. Once an investigator knows *what* they are trying to do, it is a simple task to re-identify the tools for *how* they are going to achieve their goal. As such, this book should be used as a reference manual for the OSINT techniques that have been outlined.

- *OSINT is not a silver bullet or a capability of last resort.* Just like any other intelligence collection capability, OSINT can be both successful and unsuccessful within the wider investigative practice. The key to avoiding disappointment is to view OSINT for what it is: another investigative tool. If it does not yield a result within the context of an investigation, be prepared to use something else to achieve your goal.

- *OSINT is a changing landscape.* Almost as soon as this book is published it will be out of date. This is a testament to how quickly open source intelligence is developing with new tools, techniques and methods of good practice arising almost daily. Keep pace with these developments and adapt your OSINT toolbox accordingly; this will keep skills current and up-to-date and OSINT relevant to your professional practice.

The core concepts that this book has attempted to convey are that the Internet is a multilayered space full of nuance and colour. Concepts such as cyber geography (Surface Web), looking for the weak link (Deep Web) and the rise of the borderlands (Dark Web) are all conceptual tools that contextualise the use of more tangible tools such as meta search engines, social media aggregation tools and TOR. By combining theoretical concepts with practical tools, OSINT can produce tangible gains to almost any investigation.

Conclusion

The modern world is awash with data, with the .com boom of the 1990s seeing the Internet become the defining medium for information exchange in the twentieth century. The unpredicted runaway success of new web publishing platforms such as those associated with social media has merely concreted the Internet's dominance as the main information exchange platform for now and the foreseeable future. OSINT is the key to unlocking this domain for the purposes of investigation; however, OSINT itself is a rapidly evolving practice.

The future of OSINT lies in enhancing the analytical element of the discipline, moving it away from merely a data-collection capability to a fully formed intelligence function. Having read this book and ingested the key concepts and the way the tools are used, you, the reader, by putting these tools into practice and forging your own path in OSINT professional practice, will be helping to define what the future of OSINT will be. If done correctly then if today is the information age, via OSINT, tomorrow may become the intelligence age.

ANNEX A: TIPS FOR BUILDING A CREDIBLE SOCK PUPPET

Building a fake profile can be a tedious and time-consuming task, but tips to build the credibility of a sock puppet include the following:

- *Don't leave a profile picture blank*: nothing screams 'hastily put together fake profile' louder than a blank profile picture. Take the time to select an image that suits the legend of the sock puppet. Abstract profile images of cartoon characters and the like seem to work as well as images of real people. This can be useful if you are legally constrained from using images of another person within your profile.

- *Be female*: female sock puppets tend to be more successful at developing links and maintaining anonymity than male sock puppets. This rule seems to apply for either male- or female-dominated networks.

- *Like a lot*: many social media platforms allow a user to *like* a post by another person. Liking a lot of posts is a good way to show that behind your sock puppet is a real person and a team player. This trick allows the sock puppet to more quickly integrate into the community environment common to many social media platforms without the need to engage in lengthy and time-consuming dialogues and posts.

- *Build a sock puppet's skills from the skill sets around you*: look around you in your workplace for useful skills such as linguistic ability and specialist domain knowledge that can be incorporated within your sock puppet's legend. This can facilitate entry into closed parts of the Internet and as most communication within social media platforms is relatively banal 'banter', these specialist skills are rarely called upon or questioned once a sock puppet has been admitted to a group (hence there is not the necessity for multiple operators to be standing by behind a sock puppet).

- *Use a 'real' email address*: using a free webmail account such as Hotmail and Gmail does detract from the believability of a sock puppet, whereas using a valid email address derived from a hosted website, e.g. john.smith@Smithandsmithholdings.com, adds greatly to the believability of a sock puppet legend.

- *Be bold*: in many online communities paranoia around infiltrators runs high and any new users are treated with suspicion initially. Go with this. I have claimed I am a bumbling FBI agent on many an occasion when challenged and this approach has always defused the situation with humour.

- *Get to know cultural norms*: online communities can develop strange subcultural norms all of their own such as badges of prestige and even whole new languages. Take your time to understand these norms free from the judgements of mainstream society.

- *Inward connections to your sock puppet from other users are stronger than the outward connections that you make with other users*: not so much a method, more a point to bear in mind when conducting an operation. Materially this often translates into users who have initiated a connection with the investigator being more willing to give away information or do the investigator's bidding e.g. introducing the investigator to another profile.

Annex A: Tips for Building a Credible Sock Puppet

- *Develop a constellation of sock puppets to achieve the same objective*: sometimes in an investigation you get one shot to link to a person of interest or gain access to a certain forum. If this is the case, consider making a number of sock puppet personas to conduct the reconnaissance phase of the operation. Although labour-intensive, this approach can yield results for the most delicate of operations.

ITG RESOURCES

IT Governance Ltd sources, creates and delivers products and services to meet the real-world, evolving IT governance needs of today's organisations, directors, managers and practitioners.

The ITG website (*www.itgovernance.co.uk*) is the international one-stop-shop for corporate and IT governance information, advice, guidance, books, tools, training and consultancy.

Publishing Services

IT Governance Publishing (ITGP) is the world's leading IT-GRC publishing imprint that is wholly owned by IT Governance Ltd.

With books and tools covering all IT governance, risk and compliance frameworks, we are the publisher of choice for authors and distributors alike, producing unique and practical publications of the highest quality, in the latest formats available, which readers will find invaluable.

www.itgovernancepublishing.co.uk is the website dedicated to ITGP. Other titles published by ITGP that may be of interest include:

- CyberWar, CyberTerror, CyberCrime

  www.itgovernance.co.uk/shop/p-511-cyberwar-cyberterror-cybercrime-and-cyberactivism-second-edition.aspx

- Governance and Internal Controls for Cutting Edge IT

  www.itgovernance.co.uk/shop/p-1288-governance-and-internal-controls-for-cutting-edge-it.aspx

- The Case for ISO27001: 2013

www.itgovernance.co.uk/shop/p-1158-the-case-for-iso-27001-2013-second-edition.aspx.

We also offer a range of off-the-shelf toolkits that give comprehensive, customisable documents to help users create the specific documentation they need to properly implement a management system or standard. Written by experienced practitioners and based on the latest best practice, ITGP toolkits can save months of work for organisations working towards compliance with a given standard.

To see the full range of toolkits available please see:

www.itgovernance.co.uk/shop/c-129-toolkits.aspx.

Books and tools published by IT Governance Publishing (ITGP) are available from all business booksellers and the following websites:

www.itgovernance.eu   *www.itgovernanceusa.com*
www.itgovernance.in   *www.itgovernancesa.co.za*
www.itgovernance.asia

Training Services

ISO27001, the international standard for information security management, sets out the requirements of an ISMS, a holistic approach to information security that encompasses people, process, and technology.

Implementing, maintaining and continually improving an ISMS can be a daunting task. Fortunately, IT Governance's consultants offer a comprehensive range of flexible, practical support packages to help organisations of any size, sector or location to implement an ISMS and achieve certification to ISO27001.

We have already helped more than 150 organisations to implement an ISMS, and with project support provided by our consultants, you can implement ISO27001 in your organisation.

For general information about our consultancy services, including for ISO270001, ISO20000, ISO22301, Cyber Essentials, the PCI DSS, Data Protection and more, please see: *www.itgovernance.co.uk/consulting.aspx*.

Professional Services and Consultancy

Organisations that are serious about their information security should employ best-practice security practices. Staff training is an essential component of the best-practice information security triad of people, processes and technology. IT Governance's ISO27001 Learning Pathway provides information security courses from Foundation to Advanced level, with qualifications awarded by IBITGQ.

Many courses are available in Live Online as well as classroom formats, so delegates can learn and achieve essential career progression from the comfort of their own homes and offices.

Delegates passing the exams associated with out ISO27001 Learning Pathway will gain qualifications from IBITGQ, including CIS F, CIS IA, CIS LI, CIS LA, CIS RM and CIS 2013 UP.

IT Governance is an acknowledged leader in the world of ISO27001 and information security management training. Our practical, hands-on approach is delivered by experienced practitioners, who focus on improving your knowledge, developing your skills, and awarding relevant, industry-recognised certifications. Our fully integrated and structured learning paths accommodate delegates with various levels of knowledge, and our courses can be delivered in a variety of formats to suit all delegates.

For more information about IT Governance's ISO 27001 learning pathway, please see:

www.itgovernance.co.uk/iso27001-information-security-training.aspx.

For information on any of our many other courses, including PCI DSS compliance, business continuity, IT governance, service management and professional certification courses, please see:
www.itgovernance.co.uk/training.aspx.

Newsletter

IT governance is one of the hottest topics in business today, not least because it is also the fastest moving.

You can stay up to date with the latest developments across the whole spectrum of IT governance subject matter, including; risk management, information security, ITIL and

IT service management, project governance, compliance and so much more, by subscribing to ITG's core publications and topic alert emails.

Simply visit our subscription centre and select your preferences:

www.itgovernance.co.uk/newsletter.aspx.

Lightning Source UK Ltd.
Milton Keynes UK
UKOW01f1951190717
305660UK00012B/460/P